A Culture of CHARACTER & COMMITMENT

The History of the American National Bank of Texas

A Culture of CHARACTER & COMMITMENT
The History of the American National Bank of Texas

Your Bank. For Life.

© 2016 by American National Bank of Texas

A Culture of Character and Commitment
ISBN 978-0-9845366-2-7

All rights reserved. No part of this publication may be reproduced, stored in a retrieval system, or transmitted in any form or by any means—for example, electronic, photocopy, recording—without the prior written permission of the publisher. The only exception is brief quotations in printed reviews.

Printed in the United States of America

[Contents]

Foreword 1
140 Years of Service 5
Beginnings of the United States Banking System 7
Setting the Stage: Terrell, Texas Pre-1875 9
Pioneer Bankers 17
Currency Transition 19
The Beginning: Bivins & Corley 23
Ben L. Gill, Sr. 29
Childress Brothers & Jim Harris 33
Harris National Bank–1895 41
First National Bank–1888 45
Texas Midland Railroad & Ned Green 51
American National Bank–1903 61
Ben Gill, Sr. Serves The State of Texas 67
Surviving Disaster 1929-1933 75
Walter P. Allen 81
Ben L. Gill, Jr. 99
Riter C. Hulsey 117
1970s: Seizing Opportunity Out of Chaos 127
1980s: Surviving the Flood 135
Branch Banking Arrives 141
Robert A. Hulsey 145
The Expansion of Branch Banking 155
Mike Cronin 163
Expanding the Services 175
How to Make $20 Trillion Disappear:
The Great Recession of 2008-2009 181
Board of Directors 193
Tomorrow's Opportunities 203

[Dedication]

To have grown with Terrell and having had a very influential hand in its transformation from a small village to its present standing in Kaufman County has been the privilege of this bank.

This institution is a monument to the vision of those early pioneers, but the bank has excelled for reasons beyond their efforts alone. Only through the confidence, co-operation and goodwill of many dedicated souls who have contributed to its resources over the years has this bank experienced its enviable growth and attained its present prominent standing in the banking world. It is to them then that this book is most gratefully dedicated.

We also dedicate this book to our customers, employees and stakeholders who have made the bank what it is today, ensuring our values and culture have been sustained over these many years, and will continue to be our commitment in the future.

[Acknowledgement]

The Terrell Heritage Society provided many of the photographs in this book. We greatly appreciate their efforts and generosity.

These reproduced photographs display the vibrant life of the community in Terrell. The bank was an integral part of each aspect of that life.

[Foreword]

An institution is the lengthened shadow of one man.
—Ralph Waldo Emerson

Greatest thing we can produce is character.
Everything else can be taken from us, but not our character.
—Henry Ford

The following pages are a history of an institution that has not just endured for over 140 years but, throughout them, thrived because of a foundation of character and values, and a culture of service personified by its leaders and loyal employees. It is the story of how, since the founding of this bank, it has remained intimately intertwined with the interests of the people and communities it serves. It has always been the hallmark of American National Bank to cultivate and nurture long-term relationships between those who labor and those to whom their labor serves.

Few businesses have been so closely woven into the very fabric of their communities as this bank that began in Terrell, Texas in

1875. Banking during those times required cash on hand for transactional purposes and as such, those banks were deeply imbued to their customers and their customers' businesses. They were investing in a person rather than in a business and therefore sought first a person of character. Likewise, customers often had banking choices as well, so selecting a banker was akin to selecting your business partner—someone who held high moral values, was trustworthy and who cared about your business as much as you did.

So were the times and the formation of relationship banking, and few have done it better than the American National Bank.

The character qualities of these men and women have ensured the bank's success. And these same values are embraced today by the fifth generation now in executive and management roles within this multibillion-dollar enterprise. More than anything else, those values enabled the bank to weather four of the fiercest storms in its history: the Great Depression of the 1930s, the Texas banking disaster of the 1980s, the 2001 economic collapse, and the Great Recession of 2007-2008.

Throughout its long and enviable history, these master bankers at American National Bank embodied the elements that go into making a trustworthy custodian of a community's credit and the inspiring leadership in the establishment of sound financial practices for the betterment of all. Such sterling worth and inspiring qualities of character, leadership, excellence in all they do, and service above self have been intimately interwoven with its customers, their successes and the communities served.

By forging close associations with customers, board members, employees and partners who espoused these same principles, the American National Bank has significantly expanded beyond its hometown and now services communities with branch banks throughout North Texas.

The future looks bright for this ever-expanding bank. But it all started 140 years ago in the small town of Terrell, Texas. ★

140 Years of Service

From the rural town of Terrell, Texas in the year 1875 a banking establishment emerged, providing services to assist the local community. Investing in businesses and in those communities were always the guiding principles along with:

- Excel in what we do
- Maintain the highest integrity
- Provide service above self

These are the age-old values that have guided American National Bank of Texas during our 140 years of continuous service. The most important thing about a bank is not its size in total deposits and assets. The primary obligation, through adhering to the fundamental principles in the conduct of its business, is to run a sound establishment. Of equal concern should be its interest in the welfare and development of the community through its willingness to cooperate in making loans for sound and legitimate purposes and its participation in those projects that contribute to the economic stability of the community.

American National Bank of Texas abundantly fulfills those cardinal tenets of excellent management.

Today, the bank has $2.4 billion in assets with twenty-six locations in the North Texas area. It ranks as one of the oldest banks in the state of Texas

Ever-mindful of its responsibilities to customers, employees and shareholders, the bank embarked on a successful path of longevity, serving in private ownership through five generations of a family's stewardship.

This book has been written to chronicle the rich history and heritage of this bank, its bankers and the customers and communities it serves. ★

Beginnings of the United States Banking System

President Lincoln wanted to replace the helter-skelter of notes issued by more than 1,000 state-chartered banks—a mass of paper whose value was unreliable and fickle. The belief was the notes printed by the Federal Government and circulated by federally authorized and supervised banks would restore confidence in the nation's currency.

The Congress finally agreed completing passage of February 20, 1863, of "an act to provide a national currency, secured by a pledge of United States stocks, and to provide for the circulation and redemption thereof."[1]

Thus the Government's own word was put behind the new national banks' money, which would be printed by the Government, bear the name of the issuing bank, and be

---

1   Terrell Tribune, 1965, National Bank System Dates Back To President Lincoln.

acceptable at par for most purposes, including taxes. State banks could join the system if they passed the rigid entrance examinations; a 10 percent tax on the state bank notes, imposed in 1865, later provided an incentive for joining.

On February 25, 1863 President Lincoln instituted the Office of the Comptroller of the Currency to supervise a new currency and a new banking system to go with it. Henceforth "national banks" would work with the state-chartered variety in developing the economy.

Outside Washington D.C., comparatively few people were interested in the prospects of doing business with a bank chartered by the Federal Government. Nor did this new money issued by these new banks against the security of Government bonds excite folks. The number of Americans who dealt with any kind of bank handling these notorious types wasn't very large. ★

Setting the Stage: Terrell, Texas Pre-1875

As a precursor, it may be helpful to understand the general circumstances emerging in the State of Texas and the small but growing east Texas town of Terrell where our original bank took root in 1875.

This was a time when the last of the Native Americans still roamed the plains in West Texas, railroads were expanding at an explosive rate toward the Pacific, and the country was opening up as settlers poured into the state. The lawlessness encouraged by four years of Civil War and a decade of occupation by Federal garrisons was coming to an end.

Texas was emerging from the carpetbagger regime, while struggling at the same time with problems of growth and expansion which have engaged her citizens to a greater or lesser degree ever since.

At the end of the Civil War in 1865, Texans were left demoralized, with a stunned feeling of bitterness and despair.

The economy of their state lay in ruins. But deeper humiliations and difficult struggles were ahead. The most disastrous period in Texas history had now begun and was to last for nine years … the years of carpetbagger rule. 'Carpetbagger' was a pejorative term Southerners gave to Northerners (also referred to as Yankees) who moved to the South during the Reconstruction era, between 1865 and 1877.

The term referred to the fact that these newcomers carried "carpet bags," a common form of luggage at the time (sturdy and made from used carpet). It was used as a derogatory term, suggesting opportunism and exploitation by the outsiders. Together with Republicans they are said to have politically manipulated and controlled former Confederate states for varying periods for their own financial and power gains. In sum, carpetbaggers were seen as insidious Northern outsiders with questionable objectives meddling in local politics, buying up property at fire-sale prices, and taking advantage of Southerners.

In 1865 just after the Civil War, Texas was placed under Federal military rule. Army tribunals replaced civil courts. Military commanders were given the authority to remove or replace civil authorities as they saw fit. The United States Army carried out a purge of all state officials, reaching deep down to the county level. Elections became a farce. Many southerners were denied the right to vote. Taxes were raised. Corruption abounded.

Another disaster was the fall in the price of cotton and, with that, land value collapsed.

Although these changing social and economic conditions destroyed many large plantations, the farmers in Texas were not affected much and the family farm survived. Soon after the Civil War, cotton became a major crop in the area.

Although the years of the carpetbagger rule came to an end in 1874, their impact on the political, social and economic life of Texas would last another century. Texas had acquired a strong dislike and distrust of centralized state government, and for governments at any level. These feelings also included the carpetbaggers.

The turn of the century in the United States was marked with growing industrialism and significant social changes. Population was growing rapidly. The growth of towns and cities was the dominant trend of the times. Manufacturing was replacing farming as the major source of income. Education was on the rise, closely followed by a sharp decline in the illiteracy rate. The last geographical frontiers had been eliminated with settled areas extending almost throughout the whole nation. The economic and culturally based rural family system was giving way to industrialization. In Texas, a combination of adverse economic factors, including a series of commodity price cycles, was hastening the demise of the small, family held farm.

However, in Kaufman County the agrarian life was still the dominant economic foundation. The people were hard working, independent, rugged, and not well educated. For the most part, they were pioneers, constantly seeking new frontiers, pushing back the wilderness and opening new lands for development.

Terrell, being quite remote from the larger population center around Dallas, was somewhat confined in its environs. Terrell enjoyed the more established rural structure of agricultural life rather than the commercially oriented larger cities. This provided for a stable economy and balanced growth.

Moore Avenue, Terrell, Texas 1890

In 1875, Terrell had no paved roads and no sidewalks. The kerosene lantern was the only system of public lighting. The entire south still lay dazed from the aftermath of the civil war and this depressing influence extended to small communities like Terrell.

Cotton was king and, generally speaking, the business of all meaningful commerce revolved around it. During this time there was no depositor's insurance, money was not readily available and everything depended on the conditions of the crops. The town of Terrell was sustained around this singular crop with farmers growing it, gin mills ginning it and the services of merchants supporting it. In fact Terrell was the area's epicenter of this cash crop and people came

A CULTURE OF CHARACTER AND COMMITMENT

from every direction surrounding Terrell to sell their bales of cotton.

To ensure the sustainability of this cash crop, money was needed for seed, horses and other infrastructure to plant, harvest, store, trade and transport the cotton. The need for banking facilities was urgent. It was then that the seed of the American National Bank was planted.

If cotton was the king commodity, cash was king of its citizens. During these early years, men carried large amounts of cash to transact business, whether in their boot while on horseback or in their saddlebag. Such methods of transacting business were common in the 1870s since banks were rare in the interior of Texas, and checks and letters of credit were nonexistent.

Banking in Texas in the nineteenth century was an unpopular institution. The Texas constitution of 1845 had prohibited corporate banking: "No corporate body shall hereafter be created, renewed or extended with banking or discounting privileges." This had been reaffirmed as an expression of popular distrust by the constitutions of 1861, 1866 and 1876.

A few national banks were chartered, but the requirement of $50,000 capitalization was prohibitive for most Texas communities at that time. After much controversy, it was not until 1905 when an amendment was adopted which allowed a system of state banks to be created.

But banking services of some type were needed. The economic growth of Texas in the last half of the century demanded the creation of these services. For a time, the more resourceful merchants provided credit and lending privileges as a sideline. Moneylenders began to spring up in many interior towns.

This is when private banking began evolving in the state as the sensible answer to a vital need. Men with resources

Farmers & Merchants Compress, E. Grove Street – Early 20th Century. Cotton production was the foundation of Southern agriculture and the Terrell area was no exception. This picture shows the last stage of the preparations of the product baled and ready for shipment to market.

entered the field of private banking with as few restrictions as in any other business venture. There were no established methods of operation and no regulatory body to supervise their activities. The security of their institutions was dependent on the resources and integrity of the bankers themselves.

It is noteworthy that, while banking was still developing and was still uncommon over most of the state, the young town of

Terrell attracted not one, but two private banks within its first three years.

These pioneer bankers were the forefathers of this institution. ★

Pioneer Bankers

Most early banks started as private banking enterprises. The requirements were steep. First, these brave souls needed thousands of dollars in cash before one dollar of deposits was taken in. Next, the banker had to have a personal reputation for absolute honesty. Without that, no one would be using the bank. But being honest and having the cash still were not enough. An early banker needed the good opinion of the entire community to have any chance at being successful. Finally, and perhaps most importantly, they needed an iron nerve to deal with all of the challenges of pioneer banking.

Bankers worked long hours usually as the "one man" bank. He would be the president. Then, when a customer came in he would fulfill the duties of cashier, teller, and loan officer. If need be, he would handle the bookkeeping, act as a trust officer and perhaps perform legal work if he were a lawyer. All this was not uncommon as these men did all the required clerical work.

And of course all the books were kept in long-hand, dictating many late nights.

In towns where there was no bank, money was likely to be kept on deposit with the sheriff, the local merchant, or anybody else who happened to have a safe. This often led to some unusual arrangements. Personal and political disputes could arise making the person holding all the cash a very popular figure or a very deceased figure.

The pioneer banker who survived the perils of his business tended to develop an almost patriarchal interest in his community. To a large extent, most early Texas communities eventually owed much of their later success to the bankers who honestly supervised the financial lives of these residents. ★

Currency Transition

Most banking companies were still in the hands of private bankers, and most folks demanded hard currency—gold or silver—thus depleting its value as a resource to leverage. Paper currency was in ample supply but generally disliked as experiments with paper of all kinds such as Confederate notes, carpetbagger scrip, state bank notes and private bills of hand were tried and often failed for many reasons.

As stated previously, it took men of ability and exceptional courage to start a bank in those days. Payrolls were made in silver, and the banker was required to keep on hand large amounts of specie as well as bank notes. The rise of checking was a boon to these gentlemen, for such a paper-based system allowed them to service their accounts on the books rather than in cash, ensuring hard cash could be leveraged.

While the appetite for credit was insatiable, the apparatus for channeling capital into the cotton states virtually disappeared with the tattered armies of the Confederacy. Typically, those in a position to accumulate reserves—principally merchants—organized private banks to handle loans and discounts, as they were able to begin meeting the capital requirements for credit.

The customary operations of banks of the time were based on a requirement for farm credit. Newly freed slaves and impoverished whites needed credit for seed and equipment. Moreover there was a pressing need for food and clothing, while they made the next crop. In turn, the merchant who supplied them required credit to satisfy his customer until the crop was brought in. Borrowers became depositors by the simple expedient of opening accounts, usually a condition of a loan. This permitted the bank to increase the amount of spendable funds at the disposal of the depositor without taking them from someone else. However, the ultimate movement of these funds to suppliers elsewhere also introduced a requirement for correspondent banks, which could be called on whenever the bank's own deposit and loan positions required the introduction of cash.

As private banks formulated throughout Texas, especially in smaller rural towns, issues arose from these privately capitalized banks whose circulation had been backed in too many cases by dubious if not outright spurious capitalization. Many Texans were hard hit by the Panic of 1837, which had forced the closing of banks and made notes issued by those banks worthless. By the mid-1870s banks were associated with the economic exploitation and careless overexpansion of banks, which was viewed as a major cause of the next financial crisis, the Panic of 1873. To most Texans, banks were considered a big business, which could rob the common man of his democratic rights and impoverish the unwise investor or depositor.

This public hostility toward banks deserves scrutiny because it long shaped the evolution of the Texas banking industry. The outcry from the public caused the formation of The National Bank Act of 1863 and the minimum of $50,000 capital requirement was imposed on national banks across the United States. This, combined with the prohibition of state banks in Texas, significantly spurred the growth of private banks. The scarcity of capital in post-Civil War Texas made it difficult to raise the necessary $50,000 to organize a national bank, hence the private bank proved to be the outlet for the development of a financial system. Because of these factors, the period of growth after the 'Panic of 1873' proved fertile ground to establish a private banking institution in Terrell, Texas. ★

The Beginning: Bivins & Corley

Ten years after the Civil War, the population of Texas had grown six times greater than at the beginning of that period. Terrell's downtown consisted almost entirely of wood frame buildings. The roads were dirt, lanterns lit the night and the prime modes of transportation and communication were stagecoaches, covered wagons and horses. But times were changing rapidly.

The entire south still lay dazed from the aftermath of the Civil War, and this depressing influence extended even to small communities like Terrell. People needed cash and credit to grow their farms and businesses. Real banks were needed to make this happen, and the men who ventured into providing funds for citizens would take considerable risk, uncertain if the community would welcome them. But men were certainly willing to try.

Three local citizens decided the timing was fortuitous and laid their plans to become the first banking institution in Terrell. Two years after the first map of Terrell was drawn, the predecessor of The American National Bank was opened. This private enterprise was filed under the ownership of F. A. Waters, C. M. Bivins, and John H. Corley.

On November 22, 1875, in the upstairs rooms of a building on the south side of the Texas and Pacific Railroad, these men opened their banking establishment under the firm name of Waters, Bivins & Corley, which they located in a frame building on Broad Street. The bank was the sole financial institution in the area, and people did welcome the institution.

John Corley

The driving force of the organization was Corley, a former Yankee soldier and a true carpetbagger in every sense of the word, seeking fortune in the plains of Texas. But these men were of character and leaders in finance of their day, and each destined to play an important part in the subsequent economic, civic and commercial life of Terrell.

Unlike many banking institutions of the times that frequently combined banking with other forms of business such as mercantile, commission, real estate and brokerage concerns, the original bank of Waters, Bivins & Corley was functioning solely as a private financial banking institution. This benefited their standing locally.

Though in its swaddling clothes, Terrell was then a bustling town of great promise due mainly to the fact that it was situated on the main line of the Texas & Pacific Railroad, which had just been completed through town. The railroad was the key to growth and stability in Terrell and surrounding towns and counties. With no other banks in the area, the bank was a welcome addition. From its inception, it prospered under strong leadership and soon became a very important asset to the business life of the city.

In 1876, the bank moved to new quarters in the 'Star Block' and remained there until 1882.

The re-built bank after Star Block fire, 1883

On the night of November 2, 1882, fire destroyed the entire Star Block. Fortunately, due to the foresight of the original owners and their intrepid concrete and steel bank vault, all the bank's records and securities were protected. There is no record that the bank suspended operations following this disaster, and the bank opened for business the next day. From the ashes, their new home arose on the north side of the railroad on the west half of the lot where the current American National Bank is now located.

A few years following its establishment, Mr. Waters withdrew from active connection with the bank to look after his large land holdings. Asa Holt, a man of affluence and great business talent, became connected with this institution. Soon the bank's name was changed to that of Holt, Bivins & Corley.

Like Mr. Waters, Mr. Holt's tenure was a short duration. The lure of the west eventually took him to the Abilene country. Again, the bank's name was changed to Bivins & Corley.

Even though banking entailed risks, Bivins & Corley in a thoughtful way and ever mindful of what was at stake—their customers and the communities—established a tradition that became inseparable from the bank's identity: rendering a community service or relationship banking for the betterment of all. To that end, the Bivins & Corley bankers focused on providing funds to help their neighbors and cared more about their relationships with those in the struggling frontier community than about profits, which they knew would be generated from ensuring the success of their customers. It was a timeless, value-oriented foundation: help others and in turn you will help yourself.

With this focus, they pursued a strategy that became their transcending foundation over the many years which has served the bank, stakeholders and—most importantly—their customers and communities fruitfully. Bivins & Corley soon became the catalyst for economic growth for the young town of Terrell.

The bank prospered under these men's wise leadership from its inception, and soon became a helpful adjunct to the business life of the city. It was the germinating seed, cast in fruitful soil, which has weathered the financial adversities of the centuries and blossomed into the strong and sturdy plant of the present day.

After they recovered from the 1882 fire, Bivins & Corley conducted a very successful banking business until they disposed of the bank on January 1, 1887.

Bennett Lloyd Gill, Sr.

But before they closed the bank, another character appeared on the scene. Young Bennett Lloyd Gill took a job with the Bivins & Corley bank as bookkeeper in October 1883, near his twenty-first birthday. He loved the bank business for so many reasons. He enjoyed working with figures. His honest and high integrity made him trustworthy in handling large amounts of cash. The bank's focus on helping customers and watching as they grew their farms and businesses was most likely his greatest pleasure. At the time, he had no idea what he would become.

And so it was on that day in the Fall of 1883 that the legacy of Ben Gill as a great Texas banker began eventually merging into a greater banking legacy of the Gill, Allen and Hulsey families. ★

Ben L. Gill, Sr.

Ben Gill was a native of Alabama but transplanted to Texas in his early youth, coming with his parents who relocated in Dallas. His schooling—for the most part—was obtained under the tutelage of that relentless old taskmaster 'Experience' whose only motto is, "use the rod, use it often and let it fall on the tender parts." His first employment was a general utility in a Dallas mill where he accumulated more muscle than money at a meager salary of $3 per week.

In 1875, Ben took a job at the E. J. Waldron Feed Store in Dallas where he worked hard and diligently. One year later, Ben left to work in a local grocery store, sweeping it out daily and delivering groceries. Mr. Waldron, who had moved from Dallas to Terrell to open up a grocery store, remembered Ben's energy at the Feed Store. He decided to offer him a job in his Terrell grocery store. Ben had a decision to make and it involved leaving his family's home in Dallas.

In 1879, when Ben was seventeen years old and not very happy at home, he went to work for Mr. E. J. Waldron in his grocery store. He made $15 a month, lived in the back of the store, and gardened and milked a cow for the Waldrons for his keep. Mr. and Mrs. Waldron grew very fond of Ben and for meals, often had him in their home. Mr. Waldron's brother, A. E. Waldron, became Ben's best friend and in fact was best man in his wedding years later.

Ben believed his education was insufficient and believed that to further his career he needed more schooling. Eventually, he decided to go back to Dallas and returned to school for a short time.

Since being out in the working world, he had figured out his own methods of arithmetic. He soon discovered that school was going too slowly for him. In his classes he was older and much taller than the other students, which probably added to his unhappiness with the situation. His determination to apply himself to his books might have prevailed, but for the fact that Baker B. Hoskins, of the firm Webb and Hoskins (a dry goods merchant from Terrell) came to Dallas one day and made a proposal to Ben. Mr. Hoskins offered him $40 a month. After only three weeks at old Professor Grove's school, Ben took the job in Terrell. His formal education would cease permanently at the fourth grade level. From this point on, he was self-taught. With so little formal education, it would make his later accomplishments in business extraordinary.

Ben continued to work at Webb and Hoskins for two years until 1882, when he was twenty years old. He then moved to Forney to manage a branch store for Mr. Jack Webb. A year later, Mr. Webb met with a tragic death when he was killed under questionable circumstances. His store in Forney burned down that same night. Ben remained for a few months, aiding in the clearing up of the Webb estate.

Soon after the tragic and suspicious death of Mr. Webb, young Ben Gill accepted the tender of a position with the Bivins & Corley bank as bookkeeper in October 1883, near his twenty-first birthday. This initiated the storied career of the man's banking legacy, which would promulgate four additional ancestral Terrell bankers sustaining 140 years of outstanding banking services to the customers and communities it served. ★

Ben Gill, Sr.

Childress Brothers & Jim Harris

It was a promising time for Terrell and its bank—primarily because Terrell now had access to the main line of the Texas & Pacific Railroad. By far, this was the biggest catalyst for growth throughout the entire area.

Picture of Texas & Pacific Railroad

Railroads did four basic things. First, railroad construction provided jobs. Jobs increased the circulation of money in the region and started a ripple of buying and selling that by 1890 had created the highest level of overall prosperity since the 1850s. Second, railroads allowed more efficient and extensive transportation into and out of the city. This ease of movement increased the volume and profitability of the merchandising of cotton and the wholesaling of goods. Third, railroad construction and the transportation it provided, once completed, stimulated the lumber industry that offered a new source of employment. Fourth, when railroad companies located their regional offices in the area, the city gained a long-term increase in jobs and an advantage in the struggle to wrest regional clout from Dallas.

In this era, banks were closely linked to railroads and to the larger cotton dealers. The railroads and cotton dealers were particular targets of farmers' ire, and often depicted as manipulating the economy to their own advantage and to the farmers' disadvantage. This image of banks as agents of these big-city outsiders who enter a community to manipulate its economy for their own gain has most influenced the ongoing attitude of Texas toward banks. Fortunately, this was not the case for Bivins and Corley's bank in that being a homegrown financial institution, and always fair and considerate to either large or small enterprises alike, the bankers focused on the character of a person, not on the business.

Businesses were organizations that did not make decisions and had no character. But the people who ran the business had character, and it was this moral fiber and compass on which Bivins and Corley focused their attention.

Even after the state ceased to be dominated by farmers, Texans continued to favor small locally owned banks and to insist on unit banks which carried out their business at one location. For most of the nineteenth century, such sentiment caused Texans to prohibit any type of a state banking system. This benefited the Bivins & Corley bank, even when competition entered Terrell.

Because the railroad-centric town of Terrell was prospering, another bank soon formed in Terrell, providing competition for the first time.

A. J. Childress

In January of 1876, three Childress brothers, Brice M., Asa J. and William T., moved from Sulphur Springs their general merchandise business and private bank to Terrell. They located the new bank in a brick building facing South Frances Street between Moore Avenue and the railroad with the bank using a back corner of the building. Under the name of Childress Brothers, they opened a diverse enterprise consisting of a mercantile, saddler and banking business. The bank was located on the south side of the block and was in the charge of A. J. Childress.

Now Terrell had two banking institutions. They both thrived as the town and businesses prospered.

After nine years of operation, a division of the property among the Childress brothers occurred. In the process, W. T. Childress assumed ownership of the banking business and moved the bank to Moore Avenue.

In the meantime Mr. Childress had associated with a business partner, Colonel Jim Harris. Col. Harris was a tough and picturesque ranchman having made his fortune in cattle. He now aspired to attain an equal measure of success in the banking business. In 1887 his ambitions along this line were put into action when he bought out the interest of Mr. Childress, who desired to move to California. Thereafter the bank became known as the Harris Bank.

Colonel Jim Harris

Often referred to as Uncle Jim, Col. Harris was a true Texas cattle baron. One could never forget the sight of his large stature, broad sombrero, and red serape draped over his shoulder as he rode his bay pony 'Pinto'. Though uneducated and only able to sign his name, he was well-loved and respected by the people for his wise counsel and judgment.

Terrell seemed especially at an advantage in the banking circles as both its city's banks, The Harris Bank and Bivins & Corley, were far above the average found in towns of this size. The Harris Bank had a well-earned reputation for conservatism, an essential factor in banking. It was also known for extending accommodations to its customers.

The officers at both banks (Harris Bank and Bivins & Corley) were widely known throughout northeast Texas as indefatigable workers, investing in the people and businesses of Terrell and Kaufman County. They were keenly aware that their own business was innately interwoven through the welfare of their clients; one was inextricably dependent upon the other. Many bankers talked the talk, but these pioneer bankers were willing to walk the walk, investing in both the character of a person and their business venture. Officers and directors alike had implicit confidence in the future of their bank and were willing to show their faith and goodwill by taking stock in any legitimate enterprise when needed, thus formulating even closer ties between the bank and their customers.

Since these institutions were not subject to inspection, they seldom furnished financial statements. Each bank was afraid to give out information for fear this data would be used against it by competitors. Banking had not reached the stage where financial information was regarded as a matter of public concern. What was a matter of public interest was solely the trustworthiness of the bank, and most importantly, that of the bankers. With or without competition, it was incumbent on Mr. Bivins, Mr. Corley, Uncle Jim Harris and their banks to ensure their character and value translated into solid leadership and instinctive knowledge regarding how to support their enterprising customers. Loans were executed with keen scrutiny, while preserving respect for trust in the integrity of their clientele. Through these business practices, the banks gained the trust of their customers and therefore expanded accordingly.

Ben Gill remained in his position at Bivins & Corley for three years until Uncle Jim, the owner of the Harris Bank (which had earlier consolidated with the Childress Bank), hired him to work for his bank. He was paid $125 a month, a princely sum in those days.

Continuing to grow in knowledge, experience, and ability, Ben became a principal figure in this bank. He quickly gained the respect and confidence of the owner, Uncle Jim, and the community as well. It was obvious to everyone that he was a young man of integrity with a bright future.

Ben Gill was instrumental in consolidating the Harris Bank with the banking interests of Bivins & Corley. Mr. Corley, who had active charge of Bivins & Corley's banking interest, was in ill health and desired to retire, and approached Ben Gill to present an offer to Uncle Jim. The offer proposed consolidating the two banks. Looking to increase his market share and eliminate a competitor, on January 1, 1887, Mr. Harris acquired the assets of Bivins & Corley. He then merged Terrell's two banks under Harris Bank and located their principal offices in the spacious quarters of Bivins & Corley.

As evidence of the probity and conservatism of Uncle Jim, it is interesting to note an unusual circumstance of this transfer.

Uncle Jim required the entire amount of deposits in the Bivins & Corley bank—a sum of $125,000—be turned over to the purchasers in actual cash, without notes or other forms of securities. B. L. "Ben" Gill had this to say about this historical, one-of-a-kind transaction, "I doubt if in the history of banking the world over, this act has ever been duplicated."

Due to Ben Gill's adept handling of this initial inquiry to Mr. Harris and handling the details of this transition through its execution, Mr. Harris was so appreciative that he made Ben managing head of the Harris Bank at age twenty-four—a position he held for almost four years before deciding to leave his job.

Soon thereafter in 1890, Mr. Walter P. Allen began his long tenure with Harris Bank and eventually American National Bank, due to the encouragement and direction of his friend Ben Gill. Ben Gill had become unhappy with the situation at the Harris Bank. Jim Harris' young son, John, had been brought into the enterprise, and Ben did not like some of his business practices and other things John was doing. In spite of the fact that John was considered the best Bible student in town, he was doing some gambling in Dallas, and at the bank he was switching assets on notes. The fact that Jim Harris was married to Beulah Childress, a cousin of Ben's wife Rena, and was the mother of John, further complicated the situation. Ben decided to leave the bank and, in leaving, recommended Walter P. Allen of Kaufman to take his place. Walter was an employee of the First National Bank in Kaufman. (In the years to come, Ben's son, Ben Jr. married Walter's daughter, Pauline.) Ben told Walter why he was leaving the bank, and in this way Walter was able to insist upon certain requirements of the bank's management before he agreed to take the job. So at twenty-five years of age Walter Allen, already an experienced banker, was well on his way toward an outstanding banking career.

It was a great association for Walter Allen, and it lasted all his life. The Harris Bank eventually became the American National Bank. Walter became a director of the bank in 1898 and president in 1913 serving in this capacity for thirty years until his death in 1943. During his stellar banking career, he skillfully guided the affairs of the bank through periods of prosperity and panic, building not only a major financial institution, but having great part in building the city of Terrell, Texas.

Pioneer Bankers

Ben Gill left the Harris Bank in September 1890 to become cashier of the First National Bank of Terrell. First National Bank of Terrell was then only a struggling young institution bidding for financial favor in the growing community. Associated with him was the late M. W. Raley, who later became president of the bank. Together they built First National Bank into a very successful banking institution. ★

Harris National Bank – 1895

The Harris Bank continued in successful operation until Harris' death on March 6, 1895. The following day a group of Terrell citizens led by J. H. Muckleroy and Walter P. Allen formed a corporation and purchased the Harris Bank. Joining in this acquisition were other influential and prosperous community leaders including John H. Corley, Oscar Price, J. E. McMorries, Robert L. Warren, J. S. Grinnan, H. H. Hickok, H. M. Cate, and A. J. Childress. These men comprised the bank's first Board of Directors.

On March 19th of the same year, this institution was renamed the Harris National Bank and was presided over by J. H. Muckleroy, president; Oscar Price, vice-president; Walter P. Allen, cashier; and T. E. Corley, assistant cashier. John H. Corley was selected to succeed Mr. Muckleroy as president, who died the year after his election and later by W. P. Allen.

All these gentlemen had been tried in the crucible of

the business world and achieved success in their respective lines of endeavor. J. H. Muckleroy, as the senior member of the firm of Muckleroy & Martin, had won success in the mercantile world. Oscar Price was likewise a merchant of renown. John H. Corley brought to the councils of the board his rare judgment and experience gained in the pioneer banking days of Terrell. J. B. Harris had experienced unusual banking

Harris National Bank Directors

opportunities under the regime of his father. J. E. McMorries, as a member of the mercantile firm of Jarvis & McMorries, had achieved notable success. J. S. Grinnan was a large landowner and an aggressive and public-spirited citizen. H. H. Hickok was a capitalist of sound and conservative judgment. Dr. A. J. Childress brought the benefit of his previous banking experience to the deliberations of the board. Mr. Warren went on to achieve eminent success as a lawyer and as a statesman; a man of large affairs. W. P. Allen, cashier of the new organization, had been teller of the Harris Bank since September 1, 1890, and had already exhibited those essentials for successful banking. These traits made him a permanent fixture of the bank for over thirty-five years, eventually bringing him the highest office within the board of directors. Assistant Cashier T. E. Corley, son of John H. Corley, had also obtained several years of experience in the Harris Bank and inherited a large measure of the business capacity of his father. He served the bank as assistant cashier for eight years, going to the Texas Midland Railroad as auditor in 1903.

From its beginning, The Harris National Bank prospered with capital of $50,000. Its assets soon grew to $400,000. The business became the dominant bank due to the financial stewardship of its executives and the fact that Terrell was expanding its economic climate. All of the funds belonging to the City of Terrell were deposited in The Harris National Bank, as were also those of the Texas Midland Railroad. The Harris National Bank had the only steel vault in the county, one of the famous Mosler Patent Screw safes. For many years these safes resisted every effort of expert cracksman leading crooked professionals to pronounce them 'impregnable'. Certainly this security was a key selling point in attracting new clients.

The first published statement of The Harris National Bank shows the balance of Loans and Discounts to have been $59,000; deposits were $107,000. The December 1899 statement listed Loans and Discounts of $193,000 and deposits of $225,000 and at the end of the century showed a surplus in this institution of $60,000. Ever since its inception, business has been satisfactory and from the increase in resources and deposits during its existence, optimism was always high. The Terrell Historical Society stated, "It is hardly probable that the directorate of any bank in the south represents more capital than this one." Full of confidence, the bank's board was predicting a still more flattering showing would be forthcoming in the years ahead.

Following that prediction, The Harris National Bank continued to enjoy remarkable growth, which reflected the confidence in and respect for its officers and directors. ★

Harris National Bank notes, 1890's

A CULTURE OF CHARACTER AND COMMITMENT

First National Bank — 1888

The Harris Bank, renamed through acquisition Harris National Bank, enjoyed the enviable status of being the sole banking operation in Terrell until 1888 when competition arrived.

Until then there were few national banks in Texas when a group of local Terrell citizens joined together to form the First National Bank.

The National Banking Act of 1863 had authorized the creation of a system of national banks throughout the country. Four were created in Texas in 1866, expanded to ten in 1870 and a mere fourteen by 1880. Many attempts were made to organize

First National Bank

more such banks throughout the state, but they failed for lack of adequate financial support.

Organized on January 1, 1888 with a capital stock of $50,000, the First National Bank through the years numbered among its officials, Mr. Ben L. Gill, Sr., later the Chairman of the Board of American National Bank, and Mr. Matthew Cartwright, known throughout the South as one of the leading financers of Texas.

As stated previously, Terrell was very blessed when it came to banking as both its banks, Harris National Bank and First National Bank, had progressed better than average in towns of Terrell's size. Harris National Bank had a well-earned reputation for conservatism, an essential factor in banking as well as extending accommodation to its customers. However, the new upstart First National struggled for financial favor over its dominant city competitor.

The new headquarters of the First National Bank was an

Interior of American National Bank lobby, 1920s

impressive building constructed around 1910 on the northeast corner of Moore Avenue and North Catherine Street; this building is still standing today.

This establishment was the sole competitor to the Harris National Bank for the next forty-two years.

Officers of both banks were widely known throughout north central Texas as indefatigable workers for the expansion of Terrell and Kaufman County. They realized that the welfare of one was intertwined with the success of the other. Officers and directors alike had implicit confidence in the future of their banks and were willing to show their faith by taking stock in any legitimate enterprise.

Ben Gill began his employment with First National Bank in 1890. Having become dissatisfied with some of the interworkings of senior executives in his previous bank, he departed and became a cashier at First National. His banking experience and expertise soon elevated him to senior positions.

Always seeking new opportunities to advance his career, Ben and a group of his associates were considering starting a new national bank in Terrell. To Mr. Gill, the prosperous town of Terrell seemed ripe for a third bank, and ownership certainly was desirous. When the senior management at the First National Bank in Terrell (still a young institution) learned of his intention, they approached Mr. Gill's group with a proposition they buy First National Bank. Mr. Gill, M. W. Raley and Matthew Cartwright joined forces and purchased First National Bank.

Ben Gill continued to advance his banking expertise through the positions of cashier and then as vice-president. Matthew Cartwright served as the first president and was succeeded by M. W. Raley upon Mr. Cartwright's retirement. Together they made a remarkable success of First National.

But it was not all a bed of roses. The bankers faced their first major crisis with the national Panic of 1907, a disastrous confluence of events whereby U.S. capital reserves in Manhattan banks, coupled with an overvaluation of copper stocks, had triggered a run on those banks. A nationwide capital shortage and panic ensued. Fortunately the bank had enough cash on hand to cover all withdrawals. Before the dawn of 1908, public confidence in the local money supply had been restored, and the panic was quelled.

After that, these Terrell bankers were ever more diligent in their loan allocations. In the decades ahead, their foresight to anticipate trouble and confront it preemptively became another hallmark of this bank which saved it from pending disasters as other less well funded banks toppled. Their solid core values of insuring financial integrity more than profits, and making money for their customers above making money for their institutions, continued to reinforce the bedrock of their success.

Other difficult times occurred during the 1920s, an era troublesome for many of the banks of the country. The prosperity of the years after World War I had burst like a bubble. The most serious issue for the banks in Texas during the depression of 1921 was the collapse of farm prices. Terrell had been largely dependent on cotton for its prosperity, and the bottom fell out of the cotton market.

Due to these conditions, First National Bank was never able to recover from these financial difficulties brought on by this national catastrophe. When the stock market crash came in 1929, the die was cast. It needed to find a suitor and fortuitously, their competitor, American National Bank, was able to rescue them by merging these banking institutions. ★

A CULTURE OF CHARACTER AND COMMITMENT

First National Bank, 1912

Texas Midland Railroad & Ned Green

The prosperity of Terrell and its environs can be attributed to many factors but certainly a primary influence was the expansion of the Texas Midland Railroad and its president, Edward (Ned) Howland Robertson Green (commonly abbreviated as E. H.R. Green).

Ned's mother, Hetty Green, also known as "The Witch of Wall Street", and one of the wealthiest women of her time, had accumulated a vast fortune buying railroads, as well as investing in Wall Street.

In one of her transactions, she had acquired a considerable block of bonds in the Texas Central Line. In the early 1880s, the owners of the Houston and Texas Central had begun building the Texas Midland railway. But the railroad was undercapitalized and the bondholders gathered to liquidate the assets in order to salvage whatever they could. In a complicated and long

Hetty Green,
"The Witch of Wall Street"

drawn out receivership with C. P. Huntington, Texas Midland was acquired by Hetty Green, the ever-astute business person and the railroad magnate. Hetty, through her son, offered to pay $75,000 finally securing a portion and surrendered her claim on Texas Central in return for the northeastern branch of the Texas Central—the Texas Midland portion of fifty-two miles of track running from Garrett in Ellis County to Roberts in Hunt County.

This move was primarily to protect her holdings but also to give Ned the opportunity to prove to his mother that he could manage a rail operation and thus hopefully, improve his stature to her. But it was a challenging task.

Mrs. Green sent her son, the flamboyant Ned Green, to Terrell to manage this railroad. In 1892, at the age of twenty-four, Mr. Green arrived in Terrell. He at once began his duties organizing the newly acquired railroad.

Soon after his arrival, he began consideration and discussion of locating railroad shops in Terrell. This would be a boom for Terrell and secure Ned Green as a customer for Harris National Bank. A mass meeting was held and Col. Green said he would locate his shops there if Terrell would furnish the shops site.

Seizing the opportunity, a committee was quickly appointed, composed of Major J. S. Grinnan, John H. Corley and Ben L. Gill, Sr., to seek funds for this site. Upon the parties' agreement, money was acquired and the shops built.

With this matter settled, the first public act of the new president of Texas Midland turned Terrell on its fiscal ear and opened everyone's eyes.

The always-splashy Ned Green entered the Harris National Bank and without any prior announcement, presented a check signed by his mother for deposit to his personal credit for $500,000. This was a typical tactic of the infamous Hetty Green. She believed that money talked, and putting a large deposit into the bank spoke volumes. That move gave Texas Midland, and mostly its president, Colonel Ned Green, immediate recognition and stature. It made a huge statement that big things were about to happen for Texas Midland, the city of Terrell and his bank, Harris National Bank.

Texas Midland Railroad rail shops

This certainly got the attention of the bank, as it was twice the total resources of the bank. It was a good thing that he did not ask for cash upon this deposit, and soon Hetty Green's bankers wired money on which the check was drawn. However, the bank officials wanted some type of identification from these east coast bankers. Their reply was that Ned had a large mole on his forehead, and when he removed his hat, it was later confirmed that in fact this was Ned Green. Once his mole-identification was confirmed, the money was transferred.

Ned Green

This one deposit more than doubled the assets of the bank. Because of his relationship with his bankers and his significant financial relationship with his new bankers, Green was made a director of the bank in 1898.

In a town of Terrell's size $500,000 was remarkable. As the battle with C. P. Huntington was still continuing, Hetty Green warned Huntington that she was fully behind her son with money to improve the railway and warned him to back off. She may have been bluffing but it was enough financial force to scare him off. Huntington realized that he did not want to engage in a battle that would damage his business exposure, nor his fortune.

Texas Midland Railroad was a broken-down line, in need of much repair. It was a decrepit piece of railroad. Engines were rusty, boilers leaked, rail cars were in major disrepair with the sky visible through holes in the roofs, and vegetation grew on the lines. Its infrequent passenger trains rarely departed or arrived on schedule. Yet these fifty-two miles of single line track, running from Garrett, Texas to Terrell provided Ned Green the best years of his life, and he grew in fondness for the city and its citizens.

Ned's arrival caused quite a stir in the little town because he was the only son of Hetty Green. She was a very eccentric and domineering person and Ned was glad to be away in Texas, where he was more or less out from under the constant contact with his mother.

Col. Green insisted on the latest in equipment for the Texas Midland and the locomotive pictured here is likely one such piece of equipment.

With him now free from the iron-grip of his mother, Ned was free to proceed with his endeavor and attempt to win his mother's approval. Fortunately, he had a willing banker in

Walter Allen to guide him through the many years of travail and expansion, from which they both benefited greatly, not only from the financial success, but also from their personal relationship that developed.

After Col. Green took over the railroad, he extended it to Greenville and established the town of Quinlan in Hunt County. Green then built a short line from Commerce to Paris. This left a gap of 15 miles between his roads and he made arrangements with the Cotton Belt line to operate his trains over that line between these two cities. In 1896 the northern end was completed to Paris, Texas where an outlet had connected roads from the north and east. These extensions culminated in a total of 125 miles of rail and placed it in the competitive field for northbound and southbound traffic. When he finished his line to Paris, he named it "The Lone Star Special."

It was the ambition of Ned Green to have a superbly operated and constructed rail in the state, and brains and money were used to this end without obstruction. Every improvement and advancement made in the railway science was secured for the Midland Rail, and it never was a matter of the smaller economy of saving at the spigot of the nonce and spilling at the bunghole of the future.

Col. Green had the first electric lighted locomotives and electric lighted trains in the state. He ran sleeping cars over his line that had been brought from St. Louis to Paris by the St. Louis and San Francisco. These were routed over the Southern Pacific tracks to Galveston, making possible Pullman service from St. Louis to Galveston.

Mr. Green immediately began improving and extending the railroad and sparing no expense. His policy was simply to obtain the very best, and then depend on the future for the economy.

This wise policy was fully justified by the results. The patrons of the rail line and the public generally appreciated the advanced position taken by the Midland management, and the interest on the investments produced increased dividends yearly. To sum up the splendid physical condition of the Midland Rail, it is enough to say that it was the only roadbed in the state made from prepared ballast; it had the only sixty-foot rails in the state and these weighed seventy pounds to the yard. In its mechanical department was found the finest locomotives that had ever been turned out of a machine shop, two of them being immense 100-ton, eight wheel passenger engines, built on the model of the celebrated 999 of the New York Central. No expense was spared, much to the consternation of the general public. It was a matter of common talk among people generally and railroad people in particular when President Green began his plan for wholesale improvements that "he was throwing his money away," that "the people did not demand such improvements," and that "the business would not warrant them." It was reported that on one occasion when speaking of his plans, President Green said "I want the best of everything: the best roadbeds, the best equipment, the best power and the best men I can get. If the business is not here to warrant it—it will come—and when it does I'll be ready to handle it and not have to tear up everything and rebuild." The motto of the rail might well have been "Get a patron, serve him."

Ned then relocated the railway headquarters from Ennis to Terrell and his bankers at Harris National Bank gave their esteemed customer a low-cost, long-term lease on a property they held in foreclosure. This gesture lowered his cost structure and further aligned the bank with their largest customers; a good start in the formulation of a great, long-term partnership.[2]

---

2   Terrell Tribune, April 24, 1973 "Col. E.H.R. Green and his railroad."

In later years, a railway authority S. G. Reed proclaimed, "The success of Mr. Green was due in a large measure to the splendid talent with which Green surrounded himself and to his policy of giving heads of various departments full authority and holding them to full responsibility."

Because of the close relationship with his bankers, many of them served on the Texas Midland Railroad Board of Directors, including Walter Allen, Bennett L. Gill, and L. W. Wells, among others.

Undoubtedly, his bank and its president, Walter Allen, were highly charged to commit resources to this endeavor, and through their interworking, Ned Green developed a close, personal relationship with his banker.

Although he lived in other cities, Col. Green always called Terrell his home and always cast his national political vote in Terrell. He provided guidance and strength, was a valuable asset to the Terrell community and to his bank, and performed an important part in the making and building of the city.

He always was very interested in the well-being of the economy in Terrell and organized the first demonstration farm in Texas in 1903.

The bank's association with Ned Green was a driving force in its expansion and ability to solidify his financial solidarity throughout these years. And Ned was never shy to help out when times got difficult for his friends at his Terrell bank.

Certainly his bank benefited greatly from his business dealings as well as his generosity. During the World War I Liberty Loan Drive in 1918, Mr. Green, who was now one of its directors, brought prominence to the county by subscribing a block of five million war bonds through the bank.

Ned Green taking his banker and friend
Walter P. Allen for a ride in the first car in Terrell

It was exciting to the people of Terrell to have a man of such national prominence in their midst, and they took note of all of his activities, especially in the car he drove–what many believe was the first motor vehicle in Texas! Mr. Green purchased a 2-cyclinder, horizontal type engine car from a St. Louis designer and engineer, George T. Dorris. Mr. Dorris shipped the car to Terrell and came to Texas himself to instruct Mr. Green on how to drive.

Having enjoyed Mr. Green's car, Walter P. Allen decided he should have one as well. But it was not well liked by the people of the town. This was due to the car's noise that especially upset horses frightened by its noise. All this caused a major ruckus.

Quickly, Ned became the first notable citizen of Terrell, not only because he was white, Protestant and represented millions of dollars, but because he was friendly and approachable. He fit into the Texas model and Terrell's society easily, albeit a Yankee.

But Ned had a physical handicap; a wooden leg he obtained as the result of an injury that was not properly cared for when he was a child. This disability, combined with his heritage of being in the shadow of his domineering mother, made him shun the spotlight in the past. Now in Terrell, with his mother fifteen-hundred miles away in New York City, his ego was free to expand. He took a role in a theater production and also became involved in the social scene with various organizations. The person who sponsored his entry into the many Terrell organizations and fraternal lodges that he associated with was Walter Allen. Walter became his loyal friend, a cohort mainly because it was untainted by any thought of personal gain. From the many letters that Ned wrote to Walter throughout the next forty years, it was clear that their friendship was a stable force, helping Colonel Green solidify his love for Texas and Terrell. The Allen family quickly took to Ned and did their best to match him up with likely young Dallas girls. The Allen household was totally unlike anything Ned had ever experienced—loving, kind, with hospitality that abounded. Through his trials and travails, he grew to love Texas and his banker, Walter P. Allen.

Later Col. Green went into politics and for eight years was chairman of the Republican State Committee of Texas. He was a delegate to several Republican national conventions. He was appointed a colonel on the military staff of Texas Governor O. B. Colquitt.

Upon the death of his mother, the tremendous fortune which she had accumulated, estimated at $100,000,000, was passed on to Col. Green and his sister.

In later years, Colonel Green was asked by an east coast associate at his primary residence in Rock Hill, Massachusetts why he was so fond of Texas. Ned replied, "Well, I guess it's pretty hard to understand (for a Yankee) but I belong in Texas. That's where my friends are. I wish I was there right now." ★

American National Bank — 1903

The Harris National Bank continued its successful operation until January 13, 1903, when the Harris family liquidated its interest in the bank and the name was changed to The American National Bank of Terrell.

The bank's rapidly expanding business demanded increased capital and accordingly on June 2, 1914, the capital stock was increased from $100,000 to $200,000; the increase in stock being issued to shareholders out of the surplus of the bank. Except the first two years, it is a matter of great satisfaction to the officials of the bank and certainly a compliment to their management of affairs that since nationalization no dividend period has been passed without the issuance of the usual dividend checks. In its first fifty years, The American National Bank paid more than a million dollars in stockholder dividends. At the present time, included among its stockholders are descendants of the original founders of the little bank on the Star Block.

Moore Avenue Carnival, 1907
Tents on the sides of the street and the small Ferris wheel at left center indicate that a carnival was in progress when this picture was taken.
Dirt streets and horse drawn vehicle traffic meant a far slower paced Moore Avenue than the one we know today!

The remaining history of this institution deals largely with the introduction of new faces into the official family caused by the inroads of death. Mr. Muckleroy, the first president, died the year following his election to that office, and John H. Corley was elected to succeed him. He served until his death in 1913, when W. P. Allen was elected to the presidency of The American National Bank and served in that capacity for thirty years. A born leader, as well as an astute businessman, Mr. Allen had faultless integrity and seasoned experience. He applied those traits in conjunction with sound principles of banking policy to bring honor to the name of The American National Bank. Possessing a vigorous civic pride, Mr. Allen was instrumental in bringing about many improvements, which added to the steady growth of Terrell.

Oscar Price served as first chairman of the board, an office

A CULTURE OF CHARACTER AND COMMITMENT

North side of Moore Avenue between Virginia and Adelaide during cotton season, early 1900s. The unpaved street and only one automobile of early vintage dates this picture. A portion of the American National Bank is visible at extreme right.

created in 1913. Mr. Price served until his death in 1921. There was a lapse of two years during which this office was unoccupied. However in 1923 the office was revived and Ben Gill, formerly of the First National Bank of Terrell and later with the Seaboard National of New York, was chosen to fill it.

Northeast Corner of Moore Avenue & Frances Street, 1912. The corner drug store was becoming an American retail and commercial institution by the time of this picture in 1912. As evidenced by the number visible, the automobile had begun to take a prominent place on the streets and roads of the nation.

Since the nationalization of the bank in 1895, vacancies occasioned on the board of directors by death or voluntary retirement brought about many changes in the personnel of the directorate. J. C. Maples of Kaufman, reputed as one of the ablest financiers of the county, was elected to the directorate in 1896 and served until his death in 1898. E. H. R. Green, president of the Texas Midland Railroad, H. M. Cate, lawyer and jurist, and W. P. Allen came to the board in 1898. Judge Cate died in 1905. T. E. Corley and R.

Board of Directors 1925

Jarvis became directors in 1902. Mr. Corley retired in 1924. A new face, D. M. Purvine, appeared on the board in 1905. J. C. Fields served on the board from 1913 until his death in 1916. P. J. Manning, former president of the Terrell Cotton Oil Co., served as director from 1915 until 1922, when he retired. B. E. Overton and W. C. McCord were received in 1921. Two new members, M. C. Cartwright and W. Charlton Griffith, were elected to the board in 1921. Ben Gill was elected to membership in 1923 and Ben Allen in 1925, which left the complexion of the board at that time as follows:

E. H. R. Green, W. C. McCord, Robert L. Warren, B. E. Overton, Ben Gill, W. P. Allen, Ben Allen, D. M. Purvine, R. Jarvis, W. Charlton Griffith, and M. C. Cartwright.

These men faithfully served and contributed in a large measure to its success. And in serving the bank, they also served the

Moore Avenue, 1911. The banner proclaiming 'Colquitt for Governor' dates the era of the picture. Oscar Branch Colquitt at one time operated the "Times Star" newspaper in Terrell and served as Governor of Texas from 1911 to 1915.

public. While not wholly a humanitarian endeavor, it is distinctly a public service institution. The bank is proud of this legacy and of its official family and entire personnel both past and present. It is particularly grateful of its large clientele of friends and patrons, without whom this history could not have been written. ★

BEN GILL, SR. SERVES THE STATE OF TEXAS

Mr. Gill remained with the First National Bank until 1911, when the State of Texas came calling.

Mr. Oscar B. Colquitt, a local politician, had been one of the organizers and a director of the First National Bank in Terrell where Ben was an officer. It was through this acquaintance that Mr. Colquitt began to admire Ben's integrity and his banking abilities.

When Mr. Colquitt became Governor Colquitt, he asked Ben to be his first appointment by becoming Commissioner of Insurance and Banking for the State of Texas. Ben was uncertain this was the appropriate career advancement as this post was financially less alluring than his position with the bank. However, there were other family considerations that weighed on him. One was that a change of scenery might help his wife adjust to the untimely loss of their son, Lloyd. Another consideration was how this governmental position would likely advance his credentials for his next venture.

Balancing those factors and others, Ben finally acceded to Governor Colquitt's request and moved to Austin.

Within two years, as a result of his work as Commissioner of Insurance and Banking for the State of Texas, Ben Lloyd Gill was the featured subject in the January issue of the Texas Bankers Record. It was said of Ben, "He took charge of a department of the state government a man comparatively new, little heard of, and of doubtful value to the state. He reorganized the department in a short time and had it functioning in such a manner as to be of real service to the banking system of the State of Texas."

However, Mr. Gill was destined not to fill out his term of office. His reputation as a banker and executive had gone beyond the confines of the State of Texas and had attracted the attention of Seaboard National Bank in New York City.

At first Ben Gill turned down their offer. But finally, the offer was made so attractive that he accepted and resigned as state bank commissioner.

When the position in New York was offered to Ben, Governor Colquitt did not want him to leave his administration. However, the Governor understood the circumstances and knew Ben had been working in his state commission at significantly less money than he would be paid anywhere else. It was an unfortunate consequence of government work.

As one can infer from the letter from Governor Colquitt, it is certain that Mr. Gill understood the need for a professional to continue servicing in such an important position. His request to the Governor highlighted the need to increase the compensation for said position to attract and retain the best talent and ensure Texas banks and insurance institutions remained stable and progressive.

It was essential to the economic stature and viability of the state and business growth in the future.

> Governor Colquitt Letter to Ben Gill:
> *June 30, 1913*
>
> *My dear Sir:*
>
> *I beg to acknowledge receipt of your letter of June 19, in which you tender your resignation as Commissioner of Insurance and Banking to take effect on July 10, next.*
>
> *I note your observation and recommendations with reference to further legislative action regarding the compensation of Commissioner. I believe it was in the year 1891, while a director of the First National Bank of Terrell, that I went to you, with another officer of the Bank, who is now at its head, and offered you the position of Cashier of said Bank, which position you subsequently accepted. Since this I have known you intimately, and your qualifications as a Banker and businessman generally. On the day of election as Governor I tendered you the place of Commissioner of Insurance & Banking. I felt assured if you accepted the position the Department which you have presided over would give me no cause for worry and trouble. I congratulate myself and the people of Texas when you accepted the position. You have made the State Banks of Texas trustworthy and dependable financial institutions, and I doubt whether the State has had in its services within the last fifty years a more competent and courageous*

business representative than you have made in the two and a half years you have served as Commissioner of Insurance & Banking.

Knowing as you do our long and intimate business association, and my personal attachment to you, it is needless for me to say that I regret your resignation. I can conscientiously congratulate the Seaboard National Bank on securing your services, and I predict for you a brilliant and successful future in the banking and business circles of New York.

Capable men are very needed in the public service. They are hard to secure, and still harder to keep, because the public service does not compensate a man as well for his time and labor as do large business institutions, and the conscientious public servant, such as you have been, bestows all of his talent and time in the discharge of his public duty, and has no time left for the improvement of his own private fortune.

You know without my telling you that you carry with you to your new home my good will and esteem, and that I wish for you all the success that I know your ability and attention to business will bring you.

Yours truly,
(signature of Governor Colquitt)
Governor

Ben Gill moved to New York City in the fall of 1913 and began his duties as vice-president and director of the Seaboard National Bank. This was a very interesting, challenging, and broadening experience for him.

A CULTURE OF CHARACTER AND COMMITMENT

The New York connection was a great honor and recognition for the job he had done for the State of Texas. While at the Seaboard National Bank, D. E. Wagoner, President of the Guaranty State Bank and Trust Company, suggested the name of Ben Gill as the man to be nominated for manager of the Federal Reserve Bank of Dallas. And there were more offers but Mr. Gill had another plan… the need to return to his hometown of Terrell.

Having served at Seaboard National for nine years and with three of their children all married and living in Texas, the Gills felt the time had come to go home to Texas.

Ben's associates in New York could not understand his desire to return to a small town in Texas after being in such a responsible position in the city. He did agree to be affiliated with the Seaboard National Bank as a director and to represent them in the southwest. For this service he was paid $10,000 per year. He held this position for them until Seaboard National Bank's merger with Chase Manhattan Bank.

Several years of service among the captains of finance in the metropolis however did not serve to wean Mr. Gill from the state of his early adoption. Like the proverbial cat, he came back to the old homefolks in Terrell, Texas in 1922.

As unusual as it may seem, and further highlighting his legendary status as a banker, Mr. Gill,

Chairman Ben Gill, Sr.

in January 1923, was elected chairman of both banks in Terrell: The First National and The American National Bank (the old Harris Bank). Having been associated with both banks in times past, it was a dilemma for him. The Texas Bankers Record Magazine told of this unique situation by saying that he had his money in one bank, his son working in the other, and life-long friends in both. He flatly refused to consider an executive position in either establishment for he had come home to rest and be free of responsibilities. Then the presidents of both banks agreed to urge him to be chairman of both banks simultaneously. At first he laughed negatively. But their earnestness finally won him over. As such, he became the only twin chairman in one town in the history of banking in the United States. He served in this capacity until his death September 30, 1935.

50th Year Anniversary brochure

It was during this time of dual chairmanship that Ben Gill was able to rescue the First National Bank in 1930, merging it into the American National Bank of Terrell.

He was also on the boards of the following enterprises: the Manhattan Life Insurance Co., the American Acceptance Corporation, the Terrell Mining Co., the Texas Midland Railroad Co., and of course, the Seaboard National Bank.

Mr. Gill had always been active in civic affairs. He served eleven years as a member of the board of managers of the North

Texas Hospital. He was a great lover of outdoor life and devoted much of his leisure time to his farming interests near Terrell.

Of interesting note was an article written in The Texas Bankers Record in a series entitled "Little Chats about Great Bankers in Texas." Quoting from it,

"Here are a few of Ben Gill's 'nevers'. He was never president of a bank. He never asked for a raise in salary. He was never discharged. He never made an important business decision without talking it over with Mrs. Gill. He never lived up to his salary limit. He never liked living in New York. He never went to school. He never faltered in fighting crookedness. He never flinched at duty's call. And he never refused to smoke, so long as it was cigars, or a pipe, or cigarettes, and there was a match handy. And, at the bottom of the column must come this sum-total estimate of Ben Gill: he knows what life is all about; he knows what he wants in the way of happiness; he has the courage to say 'no' to more fame and fortune if they do not fit his program; he knows when he is at the top of the hill; he is plainly content, and content with plainness; he has the good will of every man; he is considerate of the other's viewpoint; his advice and example are an inspiration to every struggling young man and to every clinging old man; he said good day to big business, over coaxings to stay, rather than be shown the door after his life's energies were sapped; he was succeeded. Few men have as positive a philosophy of life as has Ben Gill. No man ever came nearer carrying out his plan of happiness. His errand into the world has been fulfilled. If we spoke a romance language or lived in a Latinish country, we would cry right heartily, Vive la Ben Gill!

From the Terrell Tribune:

Salient points in the life of Ben Gill were his rugged honesty, his love of home, family and friends.

A biographer in the Texas Bankers Record says of him:

All the honor, all the glory, all the money in New York had to offer did not tempt this man away from his children, from friends of a lifetime, from a farm with Berkshires and Jerseys and poultry, from living his life as his wanted to back in Terrell. He knows the definite things in life necessary to his happiness, and he has those very things. ★

Surviving Disaster 1929-1933

After World War I, times were good throughout the country, perhaps too good. A nationwide boom in construction and real estate had set off a frenzy of overinvestment in the stock market by individuals and financial institutions alike. As history repeats itself, everyone thought these good times would be enjoyed forever, and few saw a pending disaster lurking. For the moment, concentration of banking services to ensure stability had won out over competitiveness.

The years of Great Depression were difficult for many businesses. As economy depreciated, many banks suspended operations, as did the First National Bank.

During 1930 and 1931, numerous economic weaknesses including the over expanded banking system of the area, the decline in real estate values, problems in the oil and gas industries, and a gigantic surplus of cotton, made carrying out the normal bank operations difficult and resulted in unusually high loan losses. Public confidence in banks, which had been eroded by news of banking disasters elsewhere, further declined as knowledge of difficulties in local banks became known.

In the days after the demise of the Texas Guaranty Fund and before federal deposit insurance, wary depositors stood ready to rush the banks to get their money out. Since not even the most conservatively managed bank had enough cash on hand to pay off all its depositors, a run could have driven any bank out of business. Faced with the threat of a run on their deposits, some banks chose to liquidate voluntarily, while larger, more secure banks acquired others.

In much of the rest of the country, banking conditions continued to worsen through 1933. Terrell was spared more severe problems in part because its economy had improved after 1931. But a good case can be made that the strong actions of the bank prevented trouble in later years. In contrast to the situation in many other areas, public confidence in the bank and its leaders remained high and prevented further issues.

American National Bank had not jeopardized its sound assets and liquidity for the sake of growth but instead had reinforced them while growing for the sake of stability. Doing so allowed it to weather the devastating storm of the stock market crash. However, actions were needed to avert the disaster, and the good bankers performed admirably.

On the other side, the financial stability of First National Bank of Terrell was not in a similar solid position. Because of this, the First National Bank decided to be acquired by the American National Bank.

On February 20, 1930, The American National Bank assumed the assets and liabilities of The First National Bank of Terrell, its competitor for more than forty-two years. It was an institution which, for many years, had enjoyed a large and confident patronage under the leadership of such able men as Matthew Cartwright, M. W. Raley, M. C. Roberts and S. J. Bass. This acquisition ensured that the depositors and stockholders of First National were rescued, and the American National Bank was made a stronger institution in the process.

At the time of the merger the stockholders, many of whom owned stock in both banks, decided that one strong institution could best serve the needs of the community at that most crucial period in banking history. The union has proved a happy one and through it, American National Bank has gained many valued patrons and loyal friends.

So from 1932 to 1948, American National Bank was the sole financial institution in Terrell. The bank had an obligation to the people and there was no change in policy other than to extend services needed by the people of the community.

For the citizens of Terrell, these were difficult years. Farm production and the general economy depreciated to low levels. Many banks suspended operation, including other banks in Kaufman County. Yet The American National Bank survived and grew strong under capable management and strong ownership. Still, the difficult times continued.

By the time of FDR's inauguration as president in 1933, banks had been "going under" at an alarming rate all over the country. One of his first official acts was to declare a four day "bank holiday" in hopes the respite would give the situation time to cool off. The very idea of Mr. Allen having to close his bank for any reason was infuriating. Hadn't he already proved his mettle in averting a bank closure in Terrell?

Just a few months earlier a rumor circulated on Moore

Avenue in Terrell that there was going to be a "run" on a certain bank in town the next day. Knowing that this hysteria (causing depositors to demand all their money at once) tended to catch fire and spread to other banking institutions, Allen went into action. He contacted the First National Bank in Dallas, his correspondent bank, arranging for the use of $500,000. This was the amount the threatened Terrell bank needed to cover the expected "run."

In the dark of night, Allen left for Dallas and drove home from there in an open touring car with the cash on the floorboard. His shotgun rested easily on the seat beside him! When the endangered bank opened its doors the following morning, its depositors soon realized there was no need for panic. They were being given the moneys they demanded so the "run" came to a halt. The bank was saved, Allen had protected his bank, and the Great Depression was denied another bank failure. He returned the $500,000 to the Dallas bank. After all, as he said, "It's on loan!"

Among the men who provided strength and guidance through these times was Colonel E. H. R. Green. Colonel Green came to Terrell as head of the Texas Midland Railroad, and he became a valuable asset to the community and the bank. In fact he just might have singlehandedly prevented the bank from liquidation because of his sizable holdings.

Between 1929 and 1945, other industries replaced cotton as the driving force in the local economy, and throughout Texas. Part of the reason for this reversal was the deterioration of the cotton trade. In the early 1930s, the glut in the domestic cotton market, the increase in foreign growers of cotton, and the collapse of the export market sent shock waves through the cotton industry. Cotton traders, however, were hurt even further by federal regulations that cut down the volume of cotton grown domestically and made the American price of cotton uncompetitive on the world market.

Regional banks and much of the regional economy had long been geared to the cotton-trading business. The decline of the cotton traders, happening at the same time as real estate construction slowed, could have proved devastating to the local economy. But it did not. Why? Other industries replaced king cotton as the mainstay of the local Kaufman County revenue source. With this new development, the bank quickly pivoted to ensure adequate resources were allocated to these new viable businesses.

Soon after this, in 1935, the Federal Deposit Insurance Corporation organized by U. S. Congress, provided insurance protection of depositors. The American National Bank, and other financial institutions, emerged stronger increasing their business with these new guarantees.

It could be said it was survival of the fittest, as the bank prospered continuing its storied legacy with much praise to be heaped on its next two leaders, Walter P. Allen and Ben Gill, Jr. ★

Moore Avenue, 1948

A CULTURE OF CHARACTER AND COMMITMENT

WALTER P. ALLEN

*"Investing in a person of character,
aligned to our bank's culture,
is more important than profits.
Do what is right for the right people.
All else will fall into place."*
—**Walter P. Allen**

An outstanding contributor to the banking scene in Terrell as well as the State of Texas was Walter P. Allen, a born leader and astute businessman. He came with the bank when it was the Harris Bank. Later he was a principal in the organizing group who purchased it from the Harris estate. He served as president of the bank from 1913 until his death in 1943.

Having served fifty years in financial institutions, Walter P. Allen's tenure was marked by steadfast stewardship of financial acumen based on the bank's guiding principle of customer and community service. Of particular note was his ability in guiding the bank during the turbulent financial and social times of the Great Depression. His vision and leadership enabled American National Bank to continue to prosper during his time at the helm. And as all leaders of this bank, his storied career began in rather inauspicious beginnings.

Bank Officers, 1925

Mr. Allen was a native of Texas. He was born January 10, 1870 at Mt. Enterprise, the son of Ben and Mattie Allen. His father was a noted educator of his day and his children had the advantage of parental instruction as well as training at their father's school. When Walter was seven years old, his family moved to Kaufman.

Walter was a prodigious student. By age thirteen he had read Julius Caesar, Cicero, and had started studying calculus. This was a great feat for any teenager much less a thirteen year old.

Soon Walter secured his first employment in a cotton yard at $5 per month. Later he became a clerk in the local office of the Houston & Texas Central Railroad, then operating from Garrett to Roberts.

Later still he was employed in the hardware store of J. S. Jones of Kaufman at a high salary of $25 per month. By the age of sixteen he was able to save enough money to pay his way through a business college in Poughkeepsie, New York. To get to Poughkeepsie, he rode mostly on cattle trains taking along enough lunch to last him a week.

After graduating with honors in 1888, he returned to Kaufman and began his banking career as an employee of the First National Bank where H. T. Nash was president. He remained under their employ until September 1, 1890 when he was offered a position as cashier of the Harris Bank of Terrell, which he accepted. Interestingly, he was suggested to Mr. Harris for the job vacated by Ben L. Gill, Sr., who resigned the position. Ben had wanted to leave the bank because of some of the business practices of John Harris, the owner's son, who also worked at the bank. However, Ben did not want to bring the problem of John's misdealing out in the open because John was married to Beulah Childress, Rena Childress Gill's first cousin. Knowing the facts and the problems inherent to the situation from Mr. Gill, Walter Allen was able to take care of everything before accepting the job. Since that time, he had an unbroken connection with that institution and its successors until his death in 1943.

Walter Allen

In 1895, following the death of Colonel Jim Harris, head of the Harris Bank, in conjunction with J. H. Muckleroy, Allen bought the Harris Bank on March 19 of that year. This institution was nationalized with Mr. Allen as cashier. The bank later changed its name of Harris National Bank upon Jim Harris' death.

He served in that capacity until 1913, when he became president of the bank. As an official of the bank and its directing head, Mr. Allen had the satisfaction of seeing the institution grow from a modest station to a position of great prominence and stability in the banking circles of the state.

He was one of those rare bankers in Texas: rare, not only in that he had rounded out fifty years in banking in Kaufman County, but rare in his abilities, in his sense of fair dealing with his fellows, in his sound judgment in business, in civic matters, in his upstanding character in the community, in his worth as a man, citizen and friend.

And he was a work-horse during those years saying, "I put in 20 hours a day, slept in the bank, got $50 a month salary, and often fell off the stool before the old Boston ledger at midnight, and was

A CULTURE OF CHARACTER AND COMMITMENT

up and at it at four in the morning." Many years later he would reflect back adding, "Now at 69 years of age I'm feeling the effects of those early years of hard work and confinement."

Many stories have been told about his ability to connect with customers and how he valued the character of the person more than their business ventures. 'Relationship banking' became his and the bank's mantra. There were many anecdotal illustrations.

Once, a man approached him after the war and wasn't sure what type of business adventure to pursue. Mr. Allen suggested that he become a farmer telling him he was a hard worker and he knew of some land this man could lease. The prospective farmer replied that he didn't own any equipment, to which Mr. Allen replied he would loan him the money for the necessary equipment as well as money for the first year's crop. Thirty years later this farmer retired. Mr. Allen, who had believed in his character, had given this man and his family a lifetime of work.

The financially turbulent 1930's, as if there weren't enough problems, produced gangsters who erupted on the scene with Prohibition and the Great Depression as their backdrop. In 1933 Congress voted to repeal the 18th Amendment of the U. S. Constitution, making the sale of alcohol legal again. But the reign of hoodlums in areas other than bootlegging still held the country terrified but intrigued. "Pretty Boy" Floyd, "Baby Face" Nelson, Ma Barker, "Public Enemy Number One" John Dillinger, and the Hamilton brothers were among the many who had people, especially those living in Chicago all the way to Texas, titillated by the headlines of yet another robbery.

And Terrell was prime hunting ground during the 1930s for two of the most notorious bank robbers, Bonnie and Clyde. Bonnie Parker and Clyde Barrow terrorized all of East Texas and Southern Louisiana. They began robbing local banks and Highway

80, where Terrell is situated, was their road of preference. They were well known as members of crime families and together they presented a formidable combination. So to protect the bank Mr. Allen prepared a response, just in case, and took to his own means to protect his institution.

Walter Allen

Mr. Allen had a habit of going to bed early and getting up early in the morning. Usually he woke up about 3:00 AM and would read murder mysteries until about 4:00 AM. Then, he would go to the bank, let himself in through the front door, and try to remember to lock it behind him before settling in at his trusty roll-top desk to begin his day.

There were no secrets where he was, as his car would be the only vehicle parked in front of the bank on Moore Avenue and the lights in his office could be easily seen. On several occasions in other towns, the robbers would force their way in, threaten the people into opening the vault, take the money, and lock the bank employees in the vault.

While the family worried about his safety, the bank employees were more concerned with their own because Bonnie and Clyde never seemed to be hampered by daylight! Word got around that Bonnie and Clyde were sleeping in the cemetery in Terrell at night, casing the location.

Walter finally came up with a solution he considered foolproof. He decided to protect his bank and had a blacksmith make an iron shield of ¼ inch steel about five feet high and installed it in the balcony that overlooked the lobby of the bank. A hole was cut in the sheet of metal for placement of a machine gun to fit through. And not just any gun; Mr. Allen got the biggest and best he could find—a Tommy Gun! The Tommy Gun was a popular sub-machine gun during World War II and also a preferred weapon of these outlaws. It had an automatic stack cartridge that could dispense a drum cartridge of 50 rounds in less than a minute. This apparatus was loaded and aimed directly at the front door in preparation for any onslaught by the notorious bank robbers.

Mr. Allen's Tommy Gun

Fortunately, it was never put to use. Had it been, it surely would have demolished the entire front end of the bank!

To ensure word got around about his new firepower, he would take the machine gun out to the city lake and fire it into the levee, making sure a lot of people were around to witness his ability and the firepower. Needless to say, word quickly got around and Bonnie and Clyde left the area. Mr. Allen likely saved the day, yet again.

Ever the visionary and aware that Saturdays were the prime banking day for its customers, Mr. Allen thought that installing air conditioning would provide a reprieve to farmers and their families when they came to town on Saturdays. He also hoped it would attract new customers desiring needed relief from the scorching Texas summers. Air conditioning proper was not unheard of but was associated with places like the picture show theaters or Neiman Marcus in Dallas. In 1935, Mr. Allen, always ahead of his time, hired York, an industrial firm, to install air conditioning at the bank. This was a roaring success and undoubtedly provided an influx of new customers.

Continuing along the same tradition as Mr. Ben Gill, Sr. to keep a family bond with the bank, Mr. Allen sent his son Buddy to college in hopes he too would become a Terrell banker. But it was a poor fit, as Buddy's schooling desires did not line up to financial management. He attended Rice University in Houston and played tennis there. Early on Buddy got sick and returned to Terrell. Once recovered, he decided to attend the University of Texas in Austin, along with his high school friend, where he likely majored in fun. Upon graduation, Mr. Allen hired his son as a bank teller in hopes that he would provide generational stewardship in the future. However, Buddy did not take to the banking profession, preferring to be outside in the open golfing rather than in the confines of a bank building.

Every day when the bank closed at 3:00 PM, the staff would stay behind to balance the daily activities books, but Buddy was out the door for another golfing adventure at Oak Grove Country Club to play his daily round until sunset. After that, he returned to the bank to review the daily balances.

Curious about his son's penchant for golf, Mr. Allen wanted to investigate and understand what was so interesting about this game that had absorbed his son. So one day Mr. Allen asked Buddy to take him golfing and they teed up at Tennison Golf Course. On the first tee, Mr. Allen drove his first ball into the lake, about 20 yards beyond the tee box. Wanting a do-over, he took another shot with the same results. After his third shot sailed into the lake, Mr.

Allen asked his son, "How much are these golf balls?" Buddy replied "50-cents each." He handed the club to his son and while walking away said, "This sport is too rich for my blood."

But father and son did share the outdoor passion of hunting. Mr. Allen was a prodigious hunter and had wonderfully trained bird dogs, of which he was very protective. One day when Buddy was thirteen, he joined his father at City Lake in Terrell for some duck hunting.

Unfortunately Buddy's gun backfired, and he was rushed to the hospital where they were informed that he would lose three fingers on his left hand. Walter, rejecting this prognosis stated, "No he will not. Just sew him up with his fingers in place." Mrs. Allen tended to her son's injury applying grease multiple times daily, and eventually they were straightened out. Allen did not take "No" for an answer from anyone.

There were differences in management styles between the Gill family and the Allen family. The Gills were more formal and stoic, displaying a traditional banker's persona. The Allens, especially Buddy, were more friendly and gregarious and thus it was evident that Buddy needed another career to mesh with his extroverted personality. At the encouragement of his mother, Buddy decided to pursue a different course in life. He purchased a General Motors dealership, Chevy and Buick, and borrowed the money from the bank to start his enterprise. With his Texas-sized personality, Buddy Allen Chevrolet became a successful dealership.

Likewise, Mr. Allen was equally gregarious and would often wander the streets of Terrell talking with people. Though he was a strange, eccentric, gruff little man, always a bit disheveled, he enjoyed paddling around town in his stocking feet and smoking a cigar while he enjoyed conversing with the people of

Ned Green's Luxury 'Green Car'

Terrell. This not only connected him to them but them to him.

As well, he did have other quirky issues, and many stories have been told about his absentmindedness and forgetfulness. One day Walter asked Ben Gill Jr. if he could borrow his car to drive to a meeting in Kaufman, which he did but mistakenly took the wrong car. At the conclusion of his Kaufman meeting, Walter again drove another person's car back to Terrell!

Another memorable story of his forgetfulness was when Mr. Allen was going up north to see Colonel Green, then a bank director and good friend, in Boston. Mr. Green had offered his luxury rail car as transport. Having arrived at his office and forgetting to pack the appropriate, more formal, dress attire, he found some clothes which he thought were his but actually were Walter Debous', the bank's porter. So, Walter ended up wearing these on his journey. Ever forgetful, he also had no money with him, which the bank proceeded to wire him upon his landing in Boston.

Another time, Walter went to Dallas to get money to balance cash on hand, which was something he did periodically. On one trip upon returning to Terrell with $150,000, he could not remember where he put all that money. The workers at the bank practically undressed him trying to find out where the money was! Finally, his hat was removed and there, in his hatband resided the $150,000. Panic dissipated.

His forgetfulness also affected his stomach. A tamale man would come by every day and Allen would consume a dozen during the morning and then was always curious why he wasn't hungry when he got home for lunch.

What he never forgot though were his customers, the farmers. He had a heart for them. Though a banker by day, he was equally a farmer himself, raising cattle and cotton on his sizeable farm and ranch in Gastonia. Because of his dirt roots, he was connected to his client base—ranchers and farmers—and he understood their labors and their plight, which boded well for both the bank and its customers.

On the other hand, he likely rejected many loans based on the same thoughtfulness and caring concern for both his customer and the bank. Once a man wished to purchase some land, but lacked collateral. The man offered his cattle as security. Walter rejected his offer as this was during the Great Depression and cattle were being shot, without need, due to oversupply in the market. Then the man offered his equipment. Again, inventory of used equipment was plentiful and the bank already possessed inordinate amounts of this. So without any viable collateral, Walter turned down this farmer. Tough times required tough decisions and he was always cognizant of what was good for his customers and the bank. Sometimes a rejection was best for both.

Aside from his banking interests, Walter Allen was associated with many large and successful enterprises. He was Vice President, Director and Treasurer of Texas Midland Railroad as well as a director of the Texas Interurban Railway. He had holdings in a number of large industrial enterprises in Terrell and elsewhere. He invested with a Dallas group headed by Mr. Karl Hoblitzelle, which bought oil royalties.

Continuing along the bank's tradition of leadership within the community, Mr. Allen was very active in channels other than the banking business. Much of this time had been given to public service. He served the city as alderman and member of the commission for a period of twelve years. He aided in the promotion of the municipal lighting plant and was in charge until he quit the city's service in 1912. In addition, he was a Mason, Elk, and Odd Fellow as well as a member of the Terrell Golf Club and the Baptist Church. He had been active in chamber of commerce affairs and was among the first to champion good roads as an agent for community development. The stretch of now completed twenty- one miles of concrete road over the Dixie Highway (now Highway 80) in Kaufman County was largely of his conception, the dream of years, and always the object of his untiring effort. In war times he was successful as county chairman of the Liberty loan drives in which the county always went "over the top."

Certainly his leadership at the bank was his foremost accomplishment but an argument can be made that his visionary efforts during World War II were his greatest accomplishments. Bringing the town together behind the war effort made the people of Terrell feel that they were an integral part of the world conflict. And specifically, bringing the British Royal Air Force Base training school to Terrell sealed his legacy.

About the time of the beginning of World War II, the British Royal Air Force desired to establish training schools for pilots in the U.S., as there was no place safe from German bombing in England to establish these facilities. The city of Terrell debated if they could manage the necessary requirements to bring about the establishment of a base where the English airmen could be trained. Getting wind of this, Mr. Allen aggressively campaigned for Terrell to become the first location. His vision was that this would create jobs, which circulated money thus creating economic velocity. He had a hard sell though, but persisted in working the local city and Kaufman County officials eventually creating a ground swell in the local population.

During a city meeting when this matter was brought up for vote, things were not going so well, and Walter Allen, being sick at the time, got up enough strength to attend the town meeting to speak favorably, encouraging everyone while laying out a blueprint for its accomplishment. He spoke of the importance of this training in the war effort and of how it would affect the economic conditions

Sunday Church Parade of the Royal Air Force Cadets, No. 1 British Flying Training Schools – World War II. Cadets pictured marching from the airfield (present Terrell Municipal Airport) on their way to church in winter uniforms.

of the town. The motion to go ahead with the project carried largely because of Walter Allen's leadership. It is something that the whole city got behind and this eventually produced many dividends for the city of Terrell and Walter Allen's bank.

In order to be awarded this flight operation, land was needed for a runway for the planes and housing and other buildings for the men. Mr. Allen again took leadership to find the land and secure it. Overcoming many obstacles, but resilient in his determination, Mr. Allen marshaled his connections to put all pieces in place. It was a success from the get-go and became the largest of the British Flying Training Schools.

The people of Terrell welcomed these English boys to their

The No. 1 B.F.T.S. was a unique aspect of Allied cooperation and personnel training in World War II. About 1900 R.A.F. cadets received their wings in Terrell and went on to serve King and Country in the war against the Axis.

A CULTURE OF CHARACTER AND COMMITMENT

town and to their homes. Soon the bank was frequented by many of these young men who sent money home to their families in England. Through these contacts many families in Terrell made fast friends of the boys from England. And it has been a rewarding association for many Terrell citizens as well as Brits.

But the real benefit of this air base to the city of Terrell and the bank happened after the war. At the end of the war having the airmen depart would likely have left an economic vacuum. Instead this created a huge opportunity. With the airbase now vacant, its expansive piece of land with a great runway and many vacant buildings allowed Terrell to create their first industrial park. Though it is unknown if Mr. Allen envisioned this fortuitous chain of events, it certainly is true that this created a significant growth opportunity when the Terrell Economic Development Corporation was formed using this acreage for enterprise expansion. This project benefited the entire region because with the post-World War II expansion years in the late 1940s and 1950s, many companies were looking for sizeable, inexpensive tracts to locate close to Dallas. With this land, Terrell became a desired location.

As each new company relocated their business to Terrell, the area surged with employees. This influx of people caused an economic boom for the city of Terrell as well as for all of Kaufman County. The employees bought housing, sent their children to school, shopped for groceries, enjoyed cinemas and restaurants and in turn, brought in many new customers, both personal and business accounts, to the bank. And much of the credit for all this goes to the original vision of the ANB bankers and their efforts which have lasted to the present day.

At the bank's 90th anniversary, tribute was paid to Walter Payne Allen Sr., who for half a century gave of his inspiration, talents and tireless efforts to make the institution a model of exemplary banking. He established the sound principles upon which the bank still operates.

Sadly, Walter Allen could not live forever and he died on December 3, 1943, before the war was over.

The history of The American National Bank would be incomplete without a tribute to Walter P. Allen, whose devotion to duty and excellence of deeds have inscribed themselves forever in the memorabilia of this bank.

In a 1950 publication celebrating the 75th anniversary of the American National Bank, the following remembrance was made concerning Walter P. Allen:

> *His was the vision, clear, to see beyond the present; and form dreams of pioneers to build; with firm resolve, for future years. His was the rugged faith, steadfast and fond in prairie lands and men whose daily toil wrought sustenance and wealth from stubborn soil. His was the courage, rare, stalwart, and true, to add to hallowed legends wise in kind, traditions of his own which proved in time, his own reward. His life's span was to view an institution rise from modest birth to take its honored place of trust and worth. There has passed from the walks of life in Terrell one of its most useful, lovable and influential characters.*

After he was buried in the Cartwright cemetery plot, his son Buddy noticed his mother saddened by this. Inquiring why this was so his mother replied, "I don't think your father is happy…he's buried with the Cartwrights." Buddy, wanting to ensure he 'rested in peace' and that his mother would also be at peace, had the funeral director and grave diggers remove him and bury him in the Allen plot!

A CULTURE OF CHARACTER AND COMMITMENT

Also, Terrell Daily Tribune provided a stirring remembrance of him:

In Remembrance
Walter P. Allen
1870 – 1943

"There has passed from the walks of life in Terrell one of its most useful, lovable and influential characters."
—Terrell Daily Tribune, December 4, 1943[3] ★

---

3   *Terrell Tribune, 1965, Walter P. Allen Guided Bank for Many Years*

BEN L. GILL, JR.

*Banking is a business; it is true—a public service, if you will.
But, more than these, banks are the heartbeats of a community*
—**Ben L. Gill, Jr.**

Upon the death of Walter Allen, the bank had planned a smooth transition for its next leader to occupy the void. But the town and its customers were not so sure. Terrell was highly aligned to the bank; its citizens and their business endeavors had prospered because of this partnership and the outstanding leadership during the Walter Allen era. Many in the community were worried about this transition of power. Would the bank's next leader be able

Young Ben Gill, Jr.

to grow and preserve the prosperity of the community? Could anyone fill the sizeable shoes of Walter Allen? It was unknown.

Ben L. Gill, Jr.

But what was clear was that the bank hoped its next leader would rise to the challenge and exceed it. So they elected its next generational leader, Ben Gill, Jr., who was well-schooled and prepared for the job. Soon, the bank accelerated its growth and during his term of leadership and influence, it prospered.

In January, 1944, following the death of Mr. Allen on December 3, 1943, Ben L. Gill, Jr. was elected to the office of chief executive. The guidance of this esteemed institution could not have been placed in more capable hands for, it seems, the better part of Mr. Gill's life had been spent in preparation for this responsibility. There was no change in its policy, other than to extend its services, and to continue its forthright, impartial operation with preference towards none.

A booming personality with a voice heard far and wide, Gill never wanted for words. If he was called upon at church, in a club meeting, or in a backyard social gathering, the tall, erect and handsome man who hid his age with a straight forward approach met all occasions with vigor.

Ben L. Gill, Jr. was born February 18, 1892 in Terrell, Texas. He graduated from Terrell High School in 1910. He attended Texas A&M University and the University of Texas at Austin and was a member of the Kappa Alpha fraternity. Before becoming a banker, Mr. Gill went to work as a fire insurance agent for an insurance company in Dallas.

Ben Gill inspecting a customer's cotton bales

Ben L. Gill, Jr.'s natural ability was augmented by his many connections with various banking institutions. These solidified his banking credentials and expertise. Ben began his career at First National Bank in Terrell on July 1, 1917. This had been the bank that his father had been formerly affiliated with. His parents were still living in New York then, but his wife Pauline's parents and Gill family members and their friends were in Terrell where they had both grown up.

In January of 1919, Ben went to Grand Saline, Texas, a little town east of Terrell and the site of a tremendous salt mine. He went to manage the First National Bank there, which had been bought earlier by Mr. Allen and Mr. Tom Meeks and his son, Eulie Meeks, who owned the largest share. Over time, bad health beset Eulie in the form of arthritis, so he chose to sell his interest in the bank and move

Ben L. Gill, Jr.

to California. Both Mr. Allen and Mr. Gill bought his shares in the bank with Mr. Allen making it possible for Ben to buy the stock by endorsing his note. Mr. Tom Meeks continued to act as president for a time after his son left for California, but eventually in November of 1919, he too moved to Los Angeles

When a position with the American National Bank in Terrell opened up, due to the resignation of Henry Corley who was going into the automobile business, Ben was offered a position. He began on January 1, 1920. When he started at the bank, there were only seven employees and deposits of $1 million.

In 1925, Mr. Gill was promoted to vice president and in 1944 became president of the bank after Walter Allen's death. He was named Chairman of the Board and Chief Executive Officer in 1967, serving in that capacity until 1975. During this time he kept a steady course as bank president, and it thrived.

Banking leadership qualifications came naturally to Ben L. Gill, Jr. who was born into the banking tradition. His maternal grandfather was B. M. Childress, a pioneer banker of Terrell. His

This picture was taken around 1950. Mr. Gill's office was in the front corner of the bank at Moore & Frances Streets. Many of Mr. Gill's customers were farmers and ranchers. The customer with Mr. Gill is Mr. Lewis, a Kaufman County farmer.

father, the late Ben L. Gill, Sr., had occupied positions of prestige as Commissioner of Banking for the State of Texas, as Vice President of the Seaboard National Bank of New York, and later as Chairman of the Board of Directors of The American National Bank of Terrell.

He was a man of impeccable ethics, with a fine regard for his employees and a deep sense of responsibility to his patrons and friends. He was also imbued with a touching devotion to his family, and an unparalleled loyalty to the bank whose steady course he skillfully maintained. Ben L. Gill, Jr. had proven himself worthy, in every respect, of the confidence and trust bestowed upon him.

Mr. Gill was by the book, careful, thoughtful, and always had the best intentions for his customers, employees and shareholders. This deep passion and commitment to serve others, do what is right—take the long-term approach regardless of short-term gain—had been the mantra of the American National Bank. As such, he carried on the tradition that served so many so well. His remarkable leadership as a banker became the envy of the Texas banking community.

He reviewed every loan with customers with the investigative thoroughness of a skilled interrogator, often asking customers not about the money requested but rather about their aspirations and visions. He would say, "The bank is going to move forward and loan you this money because I believe in your business, and most importantly, I believe in you."

His first and foremost focus was on the customer. It was never about short-term gains but rather on the long-term viability and desirability of his customers. When a competitor, the Terrell State Bank, opened in 1950, Ben Gill wanted to ensure that if customers moved their account over to this new bank, he was going to facilitate this in a timely fashion by increasing the bank's cash position to allow these customers' departure. Many bankers would have forestalled them, using additional time to convince them to keep their banking interests with American National Bank. But his integrity and belief in always doing what was right for his customers prevailed.

Though a man of a strong will, with intelligence and vision that enabled great leadership characteristics, Mr. Gill instilled a culture of caring and giving. He went out of his way to help customers and staff. He treated all people fairly. When times got tough, he generated respect and often fear with his forceful, booming and commanding voice. But he led during good times

Ben Gill, Jr. ledger, 1928

and bad. When the economy was down, he would tighten up the belt just enough to ensure measures were installed to quickly minimize any significant impact. Ben used to say, "You really don't know someone until you work with them regarding money issues." His customers likely thought the same of Ben Gill and the bank because they remained so loyal for so long.

He was a man of action, never shied away from a decision, and had the ability to always make the right ones. The successful operation of a bank called for more than a cold application of banking principles. There had to be, combined with the necessary business acumen, a thorough comprehension of the needs of the community as well as a generous amount of human understanding. And Ben held these characteristics in spades.

The Great Depression years were especially trying times. When First National Bank failed and its assets were acquired by American National, Ben discovered that many of their farming customers with smaller loans ($3,000 to $5,000), who held mostly small lots of land and maybe a mule, were likely to be foreclosed. Yet he knew these meager holdings were vital for these farmers. Not wishing to assume those debts, and more importantly, wanting to help these customers, Ben devised a plan to ensure the betterment of all.

The bank loaned these farmers money for that year's crop, subtracting their living expenses, and any money left over—the profit—was paid to the bank. Eventually every one of them paid off their balance, some taking up to twenty years. To this day many relate how important his help was to their family and how his generosity allowed their lives to continue.

He was a man of principle. If a loan seemed inappropriate, he made sure he justified his refusal. Once, a well-known cutting horse trainer desired a loan of $5,000 for a new horse; an investment which likely would have netted this rancher a 100% gain. Mr. Gill asked what a horse was currently selling by the pound, which was 50-cents a pound. Mr. Gill told this customer, "Then that's the value of the horse." He had horse sense and street smarts.

When asked what his greatest satisfaction out of life had been, Gill answered promptly, "It has been working with responsible and honorable people who met the issues of the day in a constructive way and who wanted to do something for others in addition to never disappointing the trust of people."

Though most of his activities and actions were visible at the bank and around the community, many of his efforts were done covertly to assist employees and those in the community. Once an employee of the bank was diagnosed with brain cancer. Mr. Gill got involved to assist and secured the financial means ensuring this person received the best care possible. That was his way–help others, service above self.

As stated previously, he was a visionary, always seeking innovative programs to further the bank's position based on a win- win approach. Prior to the 1950s, the vast majority of all loans was in agriculture and based on a one-year timeframe for a farmer's annual crop. Such short-term loans actualized smaller profits and required the customer to return to the bank annually for renewal. Ben sought an alternative solution. With the bank having established a healthy balance sheet and knowing the pedigree of his customer, Ben decided to create a loan program offering longer term loans. Ben's plan was to offer a three-year loan term to ranchers in the area. A loan on newly purchased mother cows was extended to three years, whereby each year one third of the principle was due. Not only was Ben's program insightful and creative for the times but he knew the business and the risk because he also raised cattle. His innovative approach allowed ranchers to expand their herds well into the 1960s, thus creating more revenue for his customers while at the same time expanding the bank's loan balance and profitability on longer-term loans.

With this new extended long-term program becoming profitable, it was a natural for the bank to begin offering extended loans to servicemen returning from World War II and the Korean War. American National Bank was one of the first banks to offer a 15-year loan on homes, which propelled the local housing industry. Naturally, this created a trickledown effect, which multiplied to many other supporting businesses. In addition, these returning servicemen were in demand for car and business loans. As the economy was booming at the time and as the servicemen were of less risk, it was justifiable to begin more long-term loans for their purposes.

The relationships that were developing during this time held steadfast, though many of these servicemen often moved to another city. Wanting to keep American National as their bank, these men would call up Ben and he'd loan them the needed funds based on their previous relationship.

Another first for the American National Bank was to finance mechanized farm equipment. This enabled the farmer, through use of modern machinery, to participate in a new era of row crop productivity.

In addition, during his tenure he held the staunch conviction to stand solidly behind the various programs of soil conservation, crop diversification, broiler plants, and improvements to dairy herds. It was a gratifying experience for Mr. Gill to put these developments in place, which added to the security and prosperity of its customers.

The bank also was cognizant to provide new services to support its customers, and one of the first new ventures was providing traditional trust services. This was as much a proactive strategy as a defensive one because customers were requesting new services that were not previously provided. Unless the bank offered these services, the customers would bank elsewhere. With the embedded motto to provide service above self, the bank began Trust Services in 1950. At the time Terrell banks were not offering such services, and though it was a lower margin business, demand was there. Besides, it was the right thing to do.

Though small at its inception, it expanded as brokerage services were added in 1995. Management changes provided challenges along the way, but today Trust Services is a strong business component of the bank's growth and vision to provide comprehensive offerings to their customers.

Reflecting back on the difference between his early days as a banker, Mr. Gill says, "The biggest difference in banking today and in 1917 is the supply of money to meet the demand. Back in the early days the demand for money was far greater than the supply and it had to be fairly and constructively allocated. Today the situation is exactly in reverse, with the supply equal to the demand or even greater."

Another insightful difference was back in the day the community and business was agrarian and with little diversity with all loans being made crops, farming and mules. Often the loans of the bank amounted to more than total deposits. Today with the economy of Terrell so diverse, loans span the reaches of its citizens and businesses.

Much has changed, and those many changes and advances can be attributed to Ben Gill's steadfast leadership. Maybe it was the

Celebrating American National Bank's 75th Anniversary – 1950

great institution he had behind him. Maybe it was the confidence he had in his ability to meet the challenges. Whatever it was, Ben Gill was a great leader in Terrell and Kaufman County.

Throughout the years, American National Bank has celebrated milestone years in its history. A major event was held on November 22, 1950 celebrating its 75th Anniversary.

Gill worked at the bank from 1920 until 1982. He served as President from 1944 until 1967. He continued his service as Chairman and Chairman Emeritus until 1985. When his wife died at an early age leaving him with two young daughters, he never remarried but dedicated his life to his family, the bank, and the community of Terrell.

One of the centerpieces of the bank lobby today is the bronze statue of Ben Gill, Jr. on the first floor. At the base of the statue is a quote characterizing his business and social philosophy:

Ben L. Gill, Jr. – Bronze Sculpture
(Terry S. Gilbreth, of Warrior Creek Studio in Abilene, Texas, created the bronze sculpture of Ben L. Gill, Jr. The smaller statues surrounding Mr. Gill represent the customers and the community he served.)

A CULTURE OF CHARACTER AND COMMITMENT

Banking is a business; it is true–a public service, if you will. But, more than these, banks are the heartbeats of a community.
—Ben L. Gill, Jr.

For all of his life, people were important. He valued each one with no distinction. In every problem, he looked for the people issues first. Then he solved the problem. To him, service to customers was to know them. He wanted to know their families and their dreams. Frequently, we talk about building relationships and developing information about their profile as if it were some new sales process. The reality is it was a return to the principled roots to know their customers and their needs in a more disciplined approach.

Upon the death of Mr. Allen in 1943, Ben was made President of he American National Bank in Terrell. Succeeding him was Riter C. Hulsey.

During the seventy-fifth anniversary of the bank, Ben acknowledged those employees, customers, and communities whose journey had been intrinsically linked with the bank in the following manner:

Dear Friends,

As you join with us in the Seventy-Fifth Anniversary of the founding of The American National Bank, we renew our pledge of service, friendship and goodwill; those things for which this institution always has stood.

And to you, our friends of Terrell and the surrounding communities, we dedicate this token of our sincere appreciation and our humble gratitude.

B. L. Gill, Jr.
Terrell, Texas, November 22, 1950.

Here are some other articles written about Ben Gill:

Ben Gill of Terrell knows what he is doing.

—Excerpt from Bankers Digest, A weekly bank newspaper, Volume 8, April 22, 1946, Number 19

The Man Behind The Scene – Ben L. Gill, Jr.

Ben L. Gill, Jr., is the President of the American National Bank, located at the corner of West Moore Avenue and Catherine Street in Terrell. He is a member of the Episcopal Church, The Terrell Chamber of Commerce, the Booster Club, and is serving on the Administrative Council of the Texas Bankers Association. He is the past Regional Vice- President of the American Bankers Association, his region being Texas.

When Mr. Gill is not engaged otherwise he likes to hunt,

A CULTURE OF CHARACTER AND COMMITMENT

farm, travel, read, (mostly magazine periodicals and trade journals on banking.) He likes television, sports and goes to every football game possible.

The American National Bank was established as a private banking firm by Holt, Bivins, and Corley in 1875. As time passed they purchased other private banks in Terrell; and in 1895, twenty years after the bank was founded it was nationalized, coming under the supervision of the Federal Banking System and complying with the rules and practice of a National Bank.

It is the aim of the bank to render friendly and courteous competent banking service and advice on business matters to its wide clientele of patrons and to all who come to them for service, and advice.

—The Terrell Tribune dated December 31, 1952

The beautiful Gill Memorial Park, located on Ninth Street, was the gift of Gill to the public schools of Terrell and still stands for many years as a monument to his outstanding citizenship. In making the gift, Gill provided space not only for school recreation and activity, but allowed room for a broader summer recreation of many sports. Other Gill and Hulsey family members contributed over the years by adding baseball fields and additional acreage for expansion.

Mr. Gill was active in the American Bankers Association. During 1929-1930, he was Chairman of the Fifth District of the Texas Bankers Association. He served three terms as Chairman of the Texas Bankers Association Agriculture Committee and one term on the Administrative Council of TBA. Mr. Gill served as Vice President twice and Director for several terms of the Terrell

Chamber of Commerce. He served as President of the Terrell United Fund and Director and Treasurer of the All Faith Chapel. Mr. Gill was a member of the Episcopal Church where he served as Senior Warden and Vestryman. In 1980, Mr. Gill was named the Terrell Chamber of Commerce "Citizen of the Year."

Always cognizant that the bank's longevity was determined by employees rising to the occasion, as Ben advanced in age he hoped to release the leadership reins to the next generational family banker. But who would fill that position? Ben, ever the planner, set a plan in place. Unsure it would be successful, but it was time to find out.[4] ★

Waters, Bivins & Corley	1875 to 1878
Holt, Bivins & Corley	1878 to 1882
Bivins & Corley	1882 to 1887
Harris Bank	1887 to 1895
Harris National Bank	1895 to 1903
American National Bank	1903 to date

---

4   *The Terrell Tribune, May 19, 1963, "Pioneer In Banking Circles Lists 46 Years Experience"*

A CULTURE OF CHARACTER AND COMMITMENT

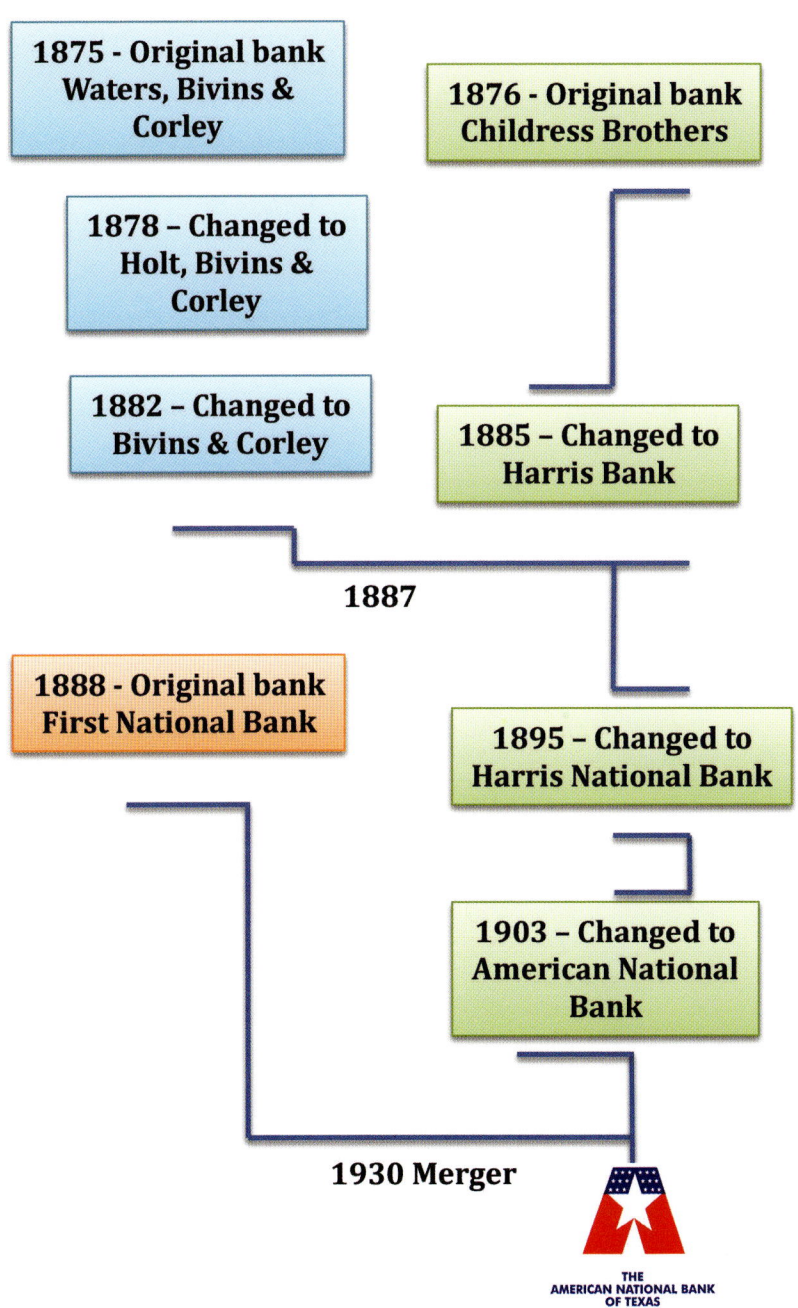

Riter C. Hulsey

Ben Gill, Jr. held the position of President for twenty-eight years, until January 1971. During this time Ben Gill, Jr. was certainly looking for his successor but never mentioned to his son-in-law, Riter Hulsey, that he might be the chosen person. Ben's only concern was that the next president was someone he could trust. Whether it would be a family member or not, it was paramount and Ben's sole focus to find the best person, one of steadfast character that had so diligently help guide the bank in years past.

But Mr. Gill certainly wanted to give Riter the opportunity to prove himself worthy. To that end, in 1947 Ben Gill, Jr. called Riter, who was working at Dow Chemical Company in Freeport, Texas, and invited him to return to Kaufman County and offered Riter a job at American National Bank. Riter reflects that, "When Mr. Gill called and asked if I wanted to work for the bank, I agreed and later realized I never asked him what the job paid. I was earning two hundred seventy-five dollars a week at Dow, and it took me three years to work my way back up to that salary," he recalls.

Riter knew he had a chance to fill the formidable shoes of Ben Gill, Jr., but he had to prove it through results. Being always results oriented, he took up the challenge and eventually proved his worth to Ben albeit a bit spotty at first. There was much to learn and time was of the essence, but Riter was determined to succeed and prove Ben had made the right decision.

After three months of "learning the ropes", Riter was given the opportunity to work as teller, and he had a lot to learn regarding the details of the business, not only regarding the position, but also about the bank's customers. On the third day of his employment, Mr. Samuels, a prominent and longtime customer, came to his teller window to cash a fifty-dollar check. Not knowing Mr. Samuels, and following procedures as directed, Riter "went around the corner to check the ledger to see if he had sufficient funds." Mr. Samuels appeared somewhat agitated by this and soon Riter found out why, as his balance held a significant position. Returning to his customer, Mr. Samuels was smiling. "I never made that mistake with him again," he laughed recalling the incident, adding, "Bank Teller is a hard job."

But making mistakes is what creates experience. Riter's watermelon debacle was one of those "valuable" learning experiences. One of the bank's customers defaulted on a watermelon crop and Riter, wanting to prove his ability in recovering the loss, decided he would take possession of the produce and sell it himself…in Chicago! His salesmanship in watermelons was a far cry from his banking abilities and though he barely broke even, it showed the board his willingness to do whatever was possible in recovering a debt. No doubt he lost his taste for watermelons, however.

At the time Hulsey began his tenure, the postings were done each morning and the ledgers were kept behind the counter with each worker having access to them. It should also be noted that there were only fourteen bank employees compared to the over 500 employees in 2015 covering all the locations.

As Riter gained experience and proved his leadership abilities, he continued advancement through the bank's hierarchy. In 1948, he was elected Assistant Vice President of the American National Bank and then cashier and director in 1949. This was followed by promotion to Vice President in 1957 and in 1964 to Executive Vice President. He was named President in 1967.

Board Meeting — Riter Hulsey on the left.

Being a born leader, as well as a concerned citizen, and following in his predecessors' penchant for community service, Riter became involved in Terrell and throughout Kaufman County. In the mid-1950s he was elected to President of the Terrell Chamber of Commerce and focused his efforts on expanding Terrell's commercial and industrial base. Much like his father-in-law, Ben Gill, Riter believed that attracting enterprises to Terrell would be essential in establishing long-term growth for the bank.

At that time it was difficult attracting industries to consider Terrell–it was perceived as too far away from the Dallas Fort Worth Metroplex with little land to develop and no incentives being offered. With this as the backdrop, Riter and the Chamber of Commerce took action and established the 'Terrell Industrial Foundation', raising seventy-five thousand dollars to allow money for acquisition of land and to build and lease facilities for industries. This proved the impetus for many companies to begin considering Terrell for their businesses and warehouses, and soon companies began moving into Terrell. This began an exciting time for the residents of the city as they looked to prosper from the promise of many jobs and growth of the community.

Maytex (now 'Madix') was the first company that utilized capital from this foundation. The only building available at the time was an old hanger facility at the airport, but Maytex was impressed with the willingness of the Terrell Industrial Foundation to assist and soon moved their operation to Terrell.

Soon, two more businesses joined the migration to Terrell. 'First Titus', from Waterloo, Iowa came to visit but the only available location was a chicken processing plant in one of the airport hangers. The excitement of the Chamber members, with chicken feathers covering them after their walk-through, sold Titus. That had to be a sight, but they were undaunted. 'Texas Aluminum' (eventually became 'Vistawall') quickly followed, relocating from Rockwall.

These three industries became very important to Terrell and this created momentum for other industries and enterprises to follow. Since their initial move, the firms have expanded their facilities and, as Riter says, "these companies have employed many of our residents and we are grateful they came." The hopes of the town had been realized.

Joining Hulsey in these efforts was Mike Cronin. Together, along with other business leaders in the area, Hulsey and Cronin continued expanding their reach and relationships. In 1985, the Terrell Chamber of Commerce established the Terrell Economic Development Corporation to further promote shovel-ready business parks, non-union labor force and pro-business leadership to companies with an eye toward expansion or relocation. It is estimated that the Terrell Economic Development Corporation has created over 3,900 jobs and added over $300 million to the local tax base.

Riter Hulsey became ANB's Chief Executive Officer in 1974 and Chairman of the Board when Ben Gill Jr. retired on his ninetieth birthday.

Riter Carol Hulsey was born December 10, 1920 in Forney, Texas. He was Salutatorian of the Forney High School graduating class of 1938. After high school he attended the University of Texas where he graduated with a Bachelor's Degree in Business Administration. He was a member of the Phi Delta Theta Fraternity and Beta Gamma Sigma, a national honor society for business students. In the fall of 1942, Riter enrolled in the Harvard Business School and was commissioned an Ensign in the Naval Supply Corps. After graduation from Harvard, Riter went to work for Dow Chemical Company in the production control department in Freeport, Texas.

On December 18, 1943, he married Gloria Gill at the Episcopal Church of the Good Shepherd in Terrell, Texas. Riter and Gloria have a son, Robert Allen Hulsey, and a daughter Carol Hulsey Yowell, and four grandchildren, Brian Gill Hulsey, Anthony Allen Hulsey, Carl Stevens White, and Gloria Lindsey White Penny.

Gill and Hulsey Families
Standing: Riter and Gloria Gill Hulsey
Seated, left to right: Carl White, Carol Hulsey Yowell
Ben Gill, Jr., Sherry Hulsey, and Robert Hulsey

Riter served on the Terrell Public Library Board beginning in 1949. He was past President of the Terrell Rotary Club and the Greater Terrell United Fund. He served on the Terrell Planning and Zoning Commission and Circle Ten Council Boy Scouts of America and Terrell Youth Center. In 1969, he was Senior Warden of the Episcopal Church of the Good Shepherd and, in 1956, was the first recipient of the "Outstanding Citizen of Terrell" award. Riter was elected to the Administrative Council of the Texas Bankers Association in 1968 and a Director of Independent Bankers Association of Texas in 1985 and 1986. He was appointed to the Board of Trustees for the Medical Center of Terrell in 1996.

A CULTURE OF CHARACTER AND COMMITMENT

Riter presided over a significant growth period for the bank during the 1960s as well as implemented innovative services and processes. American National Bank constructed the first facility that served drive-through customers on October 10, 1960. There was a walk-in area and parking space for added convenience. The motor-bank at this time had the modern conveniences of the day and allowed customers faster service. The facility was connected to the main bank building by two underground pneumatic tubes, which carried capsules holding money and/or checks to and from the main building.

The sixties marked the ninetieth anniversary for the bank and a remodeling of the main building.[5] The exterior and interior of the bank building endured many changes. The new single story addition could not be distinguished from the older structure. The west wall of the original bank building was removed so that the two buildings appear as one large building. The exterior of the building was updated with a more contemporary façade on both Moore and Catherine Streets.[6]

Riter was always a conservative banker, but yet a man of vision, which was evidenced by his decision to upgrade bank processes using computerization for customer convenience and to improve the internal processes of the bank. In 1972 the bank purchased its own computer system. This was in the very early days of the computer, and it was not easy for all to become accustomed to it. Reflects Riter Hulsey: "I really liked the old ways though, with the postings being done by hand. Now, with the advent of the computer, there are passwords and a dozen steps just to get into

---

5   *Terrell Tribune, 1965, Bank to Mark 90th Anniversary*
6   *Terrell Tribune, 1965, Motor Bank Architecture Similar to Main Building*

The new Bank building, 1965

the system. And the things are expensive too! You spend all this money on a computer system and then it's obsolete in three years."

Riter was equally focused on employing the best people, training them to ensure they developed a service-above-self mentality. With a deep consideration for his employees, he continued to hire professional people ensuring the quality of the bank's staff continued to improve. He was heard to remark, "It really amazes me how qualified and professional our staff personnel are. I'm very proud of this."

As was the success of the bank throughout its history, growth and profitability of the bank ensued from relationships developed by helping their customers succeed. As stated, "I get a lot of personal satisfaction in making loans and seeing these customers become successful with their loans. We invest in people and seeing them be successful is very gratifying. And their success comes back to you in many ways and abundantly."

During the early to mid-1970s, Riter Hulsey—first as President, then as CEO—climbed into the driver's seat and stepped hard on the accelerator. He worked to expand the bank's customer base, and with more customers came more loans, increased profits and better reserves. After several years of diligent work, the bank had a stockpile of cash which would help them expand and/or cushion any downturn in the economy.

Of course, the downturn arrived and the country was shaken to its core. But while many financial institutions foundered in the waves of the storm, American National Bank had the reserves to not only keep the bank afloat, but also position

Riter C. Hulsey

it favorably when the financial storms cleared. And that really describes Riter C. Hulsey's legacy: great when times were good and even better when they weren't. But first, Hulsey and the bank had to survive the 1970s. ★

1970s: Seizing Opportunity Out of Chaos

After World War II, the so-called "Golden Age" of American capitalism began. Economic growth was steady and occasionally fantastic, helping to keep both inflation and unemployment low. Times were good. So good in fact, that folks had the time and the money to attend a large three-day musical festival such as Woodstock in 1969. Then the first salvo hit. America's involvement in the Arab-Israeli Yom Kippur War in 1973 angered OPEC, who consequently imposed an oil embargo as punishment. Prices for a barrel of oil shot up from $3 to $12 over a four-month period, just at the time when the U.S. was accelerating its overall consumption of oil. In response, the stock market plunged and during a one-year time span, the Dow Jones Industrial Average lost 45% of its value. The result? A tremendous rise in inflation and unemployment. Sadly, the United States' economic Golden Age was being melted down and sold for scrap. Or, as someone who attended Woodstock might say, "The party's over."

So what happened to American National Bank during this time? Did they take on water and sink like so many other banks? Did they even have a few cracks in the hull? Well, when Riter C. Hulsey took over as CEO in 1974, he certainly had his share of economic chaos to face. Fortunately, in the years before the oil embargo, the bank's five key executives—Riter Hulsey, Manley Brittain—a very loyal friend of Riter's who started the Trust Department from zero and built it up by setting up trust services for many of the Terrell friends he had—Ted Garner, Guinn Godwin, and James Springer—had just begun hitting their prime. Their tireless work, ceaseless promotion and deep community involvement helped create both steady growth and a resilient culture that would help ANB weather the storm.

Each one had a part to play. Guinn Godwin was a business development expert. His technique was simple: he asked anyone he met, "Where do you bank?" When they mentioned a competitor's name, he pleaded with them, "You really need to bank with us." Rarely did he walk down the street without meeting someone and developing a new relationship.

Besides bringing in new customers, he focused hard on expanding the agricultural lending areas of the bank. This put him in touch with farmers and ranchers far and wide, many of which became long-term clients. Before long, Godwin became a household name. If a person wasn't already a customer of the bank, this massive sales force of farmers and ranchers steered them to Godwin. And once they entered the bank, Godwin didn't let them leave until he had met all of their needs, thereby creating yet another loyal client. It was an excellent game plan.

James Springer used a different technique to bring in more

A CULTURE OF CHARACTER AND COMMITMENT

customers: ethics and integrity. Springer was heavily involved with his church and other local charities. This caused him to develop close personal relationships with many potential customers. Naturally, these relationships worked their way over to a professional level. If it had to do with money, they came to James. And since he did everything in his power to make sure they were taken care of, his groups, like Godwin's, became fiercely loyal to him.

Along these same lines, but moving in different groups was Ted Garner. He also worked tirelessly to grow the business involving himself deeply in the Terrell Economic Development Corporation. This in turn, created prime connections from which long-term customer relationships developed.

For many years, these five men used their ethics, professionalism, and charm to bring in new customers and keep the bank growing. But this wasn't the only factor stimulating ANB's growth. As the customer base and loans expanded, more employees were hired. These new employees were soon integrated into the bank's culture becoming keenly aware of its mission to serve the surrounding communities. Naturally, when these employees joined civic and community organizations, they formed relationships in these groups, which also brought in new customers. New customers meant more growth, which in turn caused more employees to be hired and a self-perpetuating cycle began.

The bank's reach expanded even further when these new employees spread out to live in surrounding cities such as Kaufman, Rockwall and Canton. Eventually, there was a forty-mile radius around Terrell where the bank's brand was gaining traction in local markets. Years later, when the State of Texas legislature authorized branch banking, the bank was perfectly positioned to take advantage of this.

Prior to this legislative change though, American National Bank had been a traditional rural community bank, growing slowly but consistently over ninety-five years from 1875 to 1970. Now, with brand awareness high and customers and employees already living in the areas under consideration, the branches practically built themselves. The timing couldn't have been better. One might even say the bank was lucky, but the truth is their hard work had put them in a position to be lucky.

Automobile Bank, 1975

Once they had expanded into a number of branches, the management became aware that they'd need a strong, consistent marketing plan that would help to unify the different branches. They chose a slogan that originated from the bank's community involvement and reflected the attitude of its employees: People Helping People. And it worked—the bank grew.

During this expansion period, the bank's control structures were not keeping pace with their growth. Fortunately, the board of directors saw this and developed a better credit culture and eventually strengthened their loan processes. Declining many deals that posed unnecessary risk—even while the economy was strong—was one of the factors that kept the bank stable and out of trouble during the chaos in the years ahead. The bank's conservative

A CULTURE OF CHARACTER AND COMMITMENT

nature also helped—management believed that keeping surplus capital above the required regulatory limits was simply sound business. They knew a rainy day would come, sooner or later. And rain it did.

The 1973 oil embargo was just the first hit. In 1979, a tidal wave of economic woe crashed over on the United States. The Iranian Revolution was underway and this dramatically decreased Iran's output of oil, which the global markets were dependent upon. The markets panicked as the price of a barrel of oil shot up to $39.50. In the U.S., long lines formed in front of gas stations, and when the stations ran out of gas, people would simply park their vehicles and wait for the big truck to arrive.

All of this upheaval led to an economic condition that was so unique, it needed a new word to describe it: stagflation. Combining the words stagnation and inflation, stagflation represents a condition when there is high inflation and low economic growth. To add insult to injury, stagflation is also accompanied by high unemployment. By December 1979, inflation was at a horrendous 13.29% and a new index was created: the Misery Index. This index takes the inflation rate and the unemployment rate and adds them together. By 1980, it was at 21.98% and, with misery high, the country was falling into shambles.

And if all that wasn't bad enough, the Federal Reserve Board, deathly afraid of inflation, tightened the spigot on the money supply. That resulted in a short supply of actual dollars, right when the economy needed it most, driving interest rates up. In response, consumer spending and business borrowing slowed, abruptly sending the U.S. economy into a deep recession.

American National Bank, however, kept chugging along, continually growing and taking care of its customers. Before the second economic disaster in 1979 hit, the bank upped its game by constructing a six-lane automobile bank which was opened in March of 1975. Of course it became very popular with customers by providing faster service and more convenience.

"The capacity for individual transactions has been increased at least three times," proclaimed Riter Hulsey. "We introduced a new remote visual teller system which shortens transaction time and adds significantly to bank security. With the rapid increase in the number of banking transactions being conducted by car, we find that our customers have discovered the new facility more accessible, resulting in quicker and more efficient service."

Maybe the most telling sign of the bank's successful survival and expansion during the tough 1970s was the continued dedication and diligence of its loyal employees. The founders' belief in honesty, taking full care of the customers and putting service above self, created an important legacy that was passed on to all new employees. They, in turn, realized that living the bank's core values of integrity, leadership, passion, respect, and commitment in all endeavors was far more important than the size of the bank's deposits and assets. Their efforts and loyalty had a clear impact on the community and customers they served.

As Robert Messer stated, "To us here at the bank, it's not just a job, rather it's our life. And that's a good thing. It's allowed us to exercise our values—honor individuals and service the community—that is aligned so succinctly with our employees' personal lives as well." Or, as put in a speech to employees by Robert Hulsey, CEO of the bank:

"As an employee of American National Bank, you are part of an outstanding organization. An important component of this organization is our rich heritage. As you know, the bank began in 1875. It has survived and prospered through wars, financial upheavals, and prosperity. Even more important than its age is the system of values and culture we have inherited. The early founders built an institution that believed in the value of people and community.

People and our relationships with them are what make us who we are. They are the foundation upon which we all continue to build a great bank. I hope as each of you examines the photographs, you'll get a sense of being a part of something much larger than yourself. As you learn of the bank's history, your role is to know and then to pass it on to others so that this institution will never lose the essence of its culture and will continue to exist for years to come."

American National Bank made it through the 1970s having expanded its facilities, customer base, loan portfolio, reserves and profits. It had not only survived, it had thrived. And sure, the 1970s were tough. Real tough. But it was just a tidal wave. The 1980s were coming and would bring with it an epic forty-day flood. Could the bank and good people who worked there survive the coming storm? ★

1980s: Surviving the Flood

American National Bank entered the 1980s in a stable—but not ideal—condition. With so much growth and some underperforming loans, the bank needed to raise capital to ensure it had enough reserves. The plan was to offer additional stock at an established price to bring the liquidity and reserves up to the required level. When stock became available for purchase, the board members acquired enough shares to shore up the reserves.

Also stepping in to help was Bob Dean, a prominent Kaufman County businessman. By accumulating a significant portion of these newly available shares, Dean was elected to the Board of Directors. He understood the intrinsic value of the bank, recognized its growth potential, and set out to assist the bank to grow earnings and profitability. As an activist investor, he was outspoken on needed changes, specifically improving oversight regarding loan approval processes. As well, he had a keen eye for acquisitions and accelerated potential opportunities.

The rest of the country, though, was heading into a deep recession, taking down businesses, commercial developers and consumers. The weakest went first, and Terrell and the surrounding communities were not immune from this suffering.

The Board of Directors looked over the loans in default and others that were heading that direction, and realized they needed to stabilize their balance sheet. They had just issued new stock and this had brought in some welcome liquidity shoring up their reserves. But it wasn't enough—they needed to do more.

Don Robinson was at the helm of ANB during this time. He, along with Robert Messer, Guinn Godwin, Mike Cronin and Robert Hulsey, painstakingly dug the bank out of bad loans, bolstered the balance sheet, and implemented rigid loan approval requirements. They set up such secure practices that, if another crisis developed in the future, the bank would be on solid financial ground. This process took over two years to fully resolve itself, generating losses in 1981 and 1982. By the mid-1980s, however, the turnaround was complete bringing in good earnings through much of the second half of the decade.

In the first two years of the 1980s, two laws appeared on the books that greatly affected the fate of American banking institutions. The first was The Depository Institutions Deregulation and Monetary Control Act of 1980. This act allowed banks and savings and loans (S&Ls) to better compete for consumer savings. It quickly increased deposits, which in turn raised reserves, making more money available to lend. The act also made each bank and S&L subject to the Federal Reserve, which gave them access to several benefits the Federal Reserve had to offer.

Following this act came The Garn-St. Germain Depository Institutions Act of 1982. This gave permission to banks and S&Ls to participate in commercial real estate projects and other high-risk loans. In fact, a bank could have up to 40% of nonresidential real estate loans in its portfolio. No sooner had the ink dried on this act did banks and S&Ls begin rolling the dice and gambling on risky loans. It quickly turned into a lending free-for-all.

And then there was American National Bank. Management was still cleaning up the mess caused by the 1979 financial meltdown and did not have the will or the ability to gamble on commercial projects (unlike their competitors who popped the cork and let the good times roll). Almost all the financial institutions were out chasing fast money and by 1985 the flood waters were rising fast.

A decade later L. William Seidman, former chairman of both the Federal Deposit Insurance Corporation (FDIC) and the Resolution Trust Corporation, commented on all this, "The banking problems of the '80s came primarily, but not exclusively, from unsound real estate lending."

Incredibly, ANB was largely left out of the lending spree and while it initially looked to be a disadvantage, in the end it turned out to be a blessing. It also turned out that the two new federal acts had next to no federal supervision, allowing widespread fraud and incompetent management at banks and S&Ls, which in turn caused a banking collapse in both Texas and throughout the nation. The time had come for someone to pay the piper.

The collapse first began in the commercial sector, where so many office buildings were being thrown up. Apparently no one had considered the fact that it would take ten years worth of new companies to fill them all up. With so many vacant buildings, the only choice for a lot of them was to demolish the building to decrease the amount of available pace. Multifamily projects also ran wild, despite there being empty apartments everywhere. To fight back, the existing apartments simply slashed their rent, keeping tenants in place and assuring the new apartment projects went belly up during the first year. As more and more developers began defaulting on their office building and multifamily loans, the banks and especially the S&Ls saw the quality of their loan portfolio deteriorate, all while huge operating losses were spewing forth. With their money tied up on huge defaulting loans, they couldn't lend enough new money to dig out of the hole. As such, their financial foundations collapsed.

Another factor adding to the collapse was President Reagan's Tax Reform Act of 1986 that eliminated many tax shelters especially for real estate investments. This law significantly decreased the value of many such investments, which had been held more for their tax-advantaged status than for their inherent profitability. This, in turn, encouraged the holders of loss-generating properties to try and unload them, which contributed further to the problem of sinking real estate values.

This meltdown started primarily in Texas and the Southwest, because these areas had entered a recession earlier than other parts of the nation. Another factor that hurt Texas was the over-chartering of new banks during the first half of the 1980s, as everyone wanted in on the lending party. The fatal blow in this trifecta was the down cycle of the Texas oil and gas industry that began in 1982. All three of these events sent the balance sheets of Texas financial institutions into a tailspin. Add the lack of federal bank supervision in Texas and the Southwest (due to few bank examiners working for the federal government) and the disaster was complete. By the time the Feds staffed up to check out the books, the Texas banks and S&Ls had already struck the iceberg.

Though they had mostly stayed out of the lending free-for- all, American National Bank was not totally immune to the crisis. They did have a few bad loans here and there, but far less than it could or should have been. While most financial institutions were hiding or not answering the phone when the regulators came into Texas, ANB took a proactive approach. They worked together with the regulators to get themselves onto better footing. This turned out to be a very wise move, benefitting them greatly in years to come. Again, this strategy was directly attributable to the bank's core values of integrity and professionalism. "Our reputation as a bank that managed its affairs in high regard was known far and wide within the banking community and to the Feds," explained Robert Hulsey. While the Feds liberally scrapped bank after bank, S&L after S&L and sent bank officials to prison, the Feds, appreciating ANB's upfront approach, treated them accordingly, and kept the Terrell bankers out of the line of fire.

As Riter Hulsey said when he reflected back on the recession of the late 1980s, "We had the capital to survive. Though we had business in the construction arena with loans that went under, we were fortunate in that our portfolio of loans were not heavy in the oil drilling where many of the problems were occurring as well."

American National Bank had taken a few lumps from the disastrous 1980s, but emerged stable and strong and ready to move forward in the end. It was a testament to the leadership of the bank and the community it supported. ★

Branch Banking Arrives

Up until the mid-1980s, a bank could not have more than one location. As drive-thrus appeared, the law was clarified to allow a drive-thru facility within 20,000 feet of the bank, but no further. American National Bank had taken advantage of this rule and installed a six-lane drive-thru in 1975, which turned out to be a huge hit. But now, the economic climate in Texas was different: oil prices were in a slump and the economic recession was severe. One by one, banks were failing. This helped prompt a sudden change of heart by banking groups who had previously opposed interstate banking. Suddenly, everyone agreed that to stabilize the Texas banking industry and spur growth, a law permitting branch banking was needed. The theory was that branch banking would allow financially stable banks to expand, either by establishing new locations or by acquiring assets of those failed entities. Failed banks would hopefully turn into thriving locations and revitalize the Texas banking industry. It would be a win-win for all.

A special session of Texas legislature was called in the summer of 1986. A proposal to allow branch banking within a single county was moved through the Legislature hand-in-hand with the interstate banking proposal. The impetus for this stemmed mainly from former Attorney General Jim Mattox's ruling that a law allowing drive-thru banks located up to 20,000 feet from the main institution violated the state constitution. "This is the only state in the nation with a constitution stating a bank can't do business in more than one place," said Sam Kimberlin Jr. of the Texas Bankers Association, which represented both large and small banks. Frank Anderson, at the time a banking analyst with the investment firm of Weber, Hall, Sale & Associates in Dallas, added, "People are finally starting to realize that you can't bank in 1986 with laws written in 1904."

With all this momentum, the legislature passed an interstate banking law and approved a public referendum to amend the state's constitution allowing limited branch banking to appear on the ballot in the November election. The electorate passed the referendum and the interstate banking law took effect on January 1, 1987, allowing Texas—the largest state—to open its doors to branch banking. For the first time in its one hundred fifty year history, outside banks were allowed to come in and do business. This was a watershed moment in the Texas banking industry. "It was just something whose time had come," said Texas Banking Commissioner James Sexton, who first proposed the change in a meeting with Gov. Mark White. F. Hagen McMahon Jr., a banking lobbyist added, "The weakening financial condition and funding of several large banks and the rapid deterioration of the economy, forces Texas to seek diversification, and to do that, you need new capital."

With the ability to now expand into branch banking,

along with its solid balance sheet, American National Bank was ready to seize the opportunity. Soon after the law was on the books, ANB began to take advantage of its new condition by acquiring the assets of failing or insolvent banks in their region. Since a proviso of the legislature limited expansion only to the same county where a bank was domiciled, ANB could establish branches solely in Kaufman County. But it was a start.

The bank added its first branch in Forney, which was a logical step, as many of its customers and employees were residents. This proved to be a launching pad for ANB branch banking, an expansion that would significantly grow the bank's balance sheets for years to come. ★

A CULTURE OF CHARACTER AND COMMITMENT

Robert A. Hulsey

During the turbulent years of the 1980s, Riter Hulsey began searching for someone to replace him. His overriding concern was that the foundational values of the bank would endure far into the future. Like his father-in-law before him, Riter wanted the best person for the job—a person of character, ability and innate leadership qualities. Hoping to keep the business in the family, Riter began studying and watching his son's progress. He was duly impressed. Robert, much like his father, proved a quick study. He had shown both ability and steadfast leadership in managing the bank through multiple crises. Riter also understood that it was critically important to maintain continuity in finding the next president. Just as Ben Gill, Jr. had hoped a family member would ascend to top, now this became Riter's decision.

In late 1989, Robert Hulsey assumed leadership of the family institution. It was now his turn to take the helm and chart a strategy to grow the bank. And, like his father before him, he succeeded, both through acquisition and expansion, and by increasing the bank's portfolio of services. Also like his father, Robert faced the daunting task of managing the bank through stormy seas and occasionally righting the ship through some of the most difficult years in the bank's history. As the fifth generational leader of the Terrell bank, only time would tell if he could fill the shoes of his ancestors and continue the legacy of the American National Bank.

During the tumultuous years of the 1980s, the bankers' financial acumen and principled values were the undeniable reasons having survived and, in fact, thrived during those times.

Unarguably, one might say that the man leading the troops should be given much of the credit. But Robert Hulsey never would admit this. Always humble, he would cite his board and all the bank's employees for their dedication, intelligence, and hard work, as well as honoring a dedicated customer base among a host of other reasons.

Like his father before him, he had come a long way from his first job at the bank, learning by going through the ranks.

When Robert A. Hulsey first joined the American National Bank of Texas in June 1976, times were good. The bank's assets were growing, the balance sheet was aligned and future success was guaranteed, or so he thought.

What brought Robert to the bank was not initially a sense of generational responsibility to continue their family's banking legacy. Rather, it was a change of events within his initial professional endeavors.

Though his father Riter certainly wanted his son to continue the family legacy, he never mentioned to him that he should work at the bank; that was just not his way. Riter wanted his son to want to work at the bank. As was Riter's demeanor, he always understood that a person's decision had to be from within—without outside influence—ensuring that one's character and aspirations evolved from heart-felt desire. Success would then likely follow. In time, Robert came to his decision on his own terms, though taking a rather circuitous route.

Robert Allen Hulsey had been born May 9, 1946 in Velasco, Texas. After graduating from Terrell High School, Robert attended the University of Texas, earning a Bachelor's Degree in Mechanical Engineering. Robert also acquired a Master's Degree of Business Administration from the Wharton Graduate School at the University of Pennsylvania. After graduation from Wharton, Robert worked at Texas Instruments in Dallas in various departments including: financial control, product planning, manufacturing management and engineering management.

During his six years at Texas Instruments, there were several incidences that troubled him. "Once, I saw a thirty year employee called in to be told that his services were no longer needed. Security guards were stationed outside holding a brown box as the now former employee was being escorted out. I started to realize that my family and career path needed more security." Though he had resisted going into the family business, these acts he perceived to be inhumane solidified his decision, and he became comfortable with working at the family enterprise. "I decided that I did want to help the institution that had provided so well for our family and so many others. I wanted to make a difference, to help the bank succeed. If I didn't think I could do that, I wouldn't have made the decision. It would be different living in a small town, but I liked the idea of coming back to raise my family and I had decided I wanted the opportunity to work at the bank."

He also knew that if it did not work out he could always leave, mentioning, "I was still young and had plenty of time to still make a change if needed."

A change was never necessary and the bank prospered under his stewardship and leadership as CEO.

In his first bank assignment, he was to manage the investment portfolio. "My natural tendency is to jump in, get involved and put forward a budget where the bank might be heading financially." But first he felt the need to understand the guts of the internal bank's interworking, reflecting "I wanted to learn more about the bank from the ground level so I got trained as a loan note teller, where the customer would come in to pay their loans." Riter, being such an unselfish person, was willing to give Robert an opportunity to get involved where he deemed necessary; never directing, rather guiding, with a steady hand.

On his educational journey, Robert deemed it essential to learn the loan side of the bank, but he was a sucker for customer stories and didn't fare all too well, explaining, "Once a girl had this sob story and I fell into her trap. Overhearing our conversation was a bank loan officer with her head down, very quiet and seemed asleep. Later I asked her why her head was down during this interview and she said she was praying I would not make the loan!" That certainly taught him a lesson, and being a quick study, he rose within the ranks because of his intelligence and capability. He grew to understand his DNA was the bank, and the bank prospered under his leadership.

Robert was the catalyst for change, and his vision and stewardship led the troops on many fronts. Having started at the bottom to learn the business, he worked hard and earned his way up the ladder based on accomplishments, not on privilege.

Another trait of Robert was his ability to motivate and inspire the staff. They trusted him as he was a man of his word, and the troops followed with unendingly dedication. As Robert states, "I connect with people; I trust people and believe they trust me. I'm able to relate things instinctively, with conviction and emotion, and help our teams understand the 'why'. I think I'm effective at public speaking and have been able to lay out, with clarity, the past, present and future. I make sure people are recognized for their accomplishments and all are part of a broader team. We succeed not as individuals but rather as a cohesive group of dedicated professionals with a passion for excellence in all we do and for all we serve."

As well, he was a visionary and understood that to grow, change is necessary. He was a catalyst for that change stating, "I see where things are going, where opportunities are, and have the willingness to engage our teams, and execute our strategy and tactics."

As an example of this, he was instrumental in upgrading technology at the bank. Understanding that Internet banking was the wave of the future, but mindful that the bank's high-touch customer service was equally as important, he began implementing a combined strategy. "Technology is critical for any bank now. We see people combining the Internet with personal service for their banking needs. But no matter how easy banking by computer becomes, people will still want to talk to someone they have confidence in. They want to meet face to face. We are planning on this dual strategy to accommodate our customers," said Robert. Continuing, "We focus on people issues here. Customer service is not just a campaign slogan. We learned from generations who worked here before and will pass on to the generation to come."

He also had a humorous side. Once, Robert Messer came to request his expense money that he had submitted. At the time we were very loose in handling minor expenses for lunches and dinners, so Sue Nichols handed Hulsey the twenty-six dollars due to Messer. Hulsey soon forgot about this but Messer had not and constantly mentioned wanting his reimbursement. Every time he

AMERICAN NATIONAL BANK

requested it, Hulsey didn't seem to have any cash. Messer, becoming frustrated by this, sought recourse by taking, more like stealing, things out of Hulsey's office as collateral and to get his attention. Hulsey explains, "For a while I did not notice that things were missing but one morning when I entered my office, I was aware that many things had seemed to disappear. I was advised what Messer was up to. So, game on! We had this conference with thirty people and I had a police officer, a mountain of a man physically, enter and say in a booming deep voice: 'Is Robert Messer here? I have a warrant for your arrest for theft of office goods.' Mr. James Springer, playing to the ruse, stood up and said, 'I saw him do it!' Needing to take control of this situation before it got out of hand, I asked for a vote if anyone would stand for his good character. Not a single person would vouch for Robert Messer as they all were playing along. Robert finally realized the joke was on him stating, "I think I have been had!"

On January 1, 1979, Hulsey was promoted to Vice President and to Senior Vice President of Lending on March 1, 1984. He then became Executive Vice President of Operations on January 1, 1988, and Chief Executive Officer on October 17, 1989.

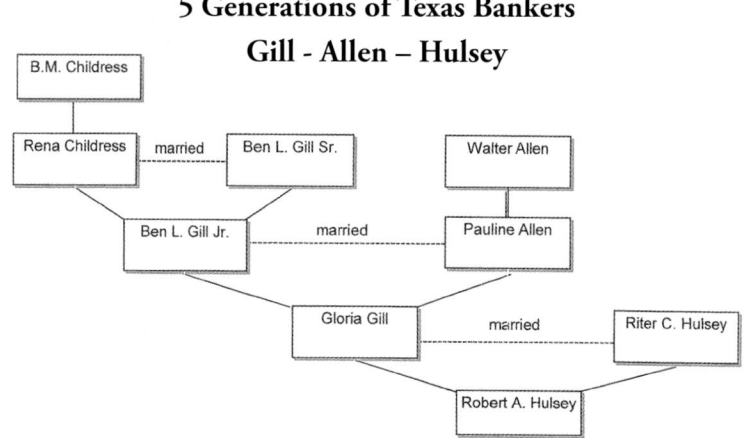

**5 Generations of Texas Bankers
Gill - Allen – Hulsey**

A CULTURE OF CHARACTER AND COMMITMENT

As a benchmark of his leadership, the results speak volumes. Based on his principled axiom to run a sound financial institution and to strengthen those communities it serves, the bank thrived under his stewardship.

As Robert states, "The most important thing about a bank is not its size in total deposits and assets. The primary obligation, through adhering to the fundamental principles in the conduct of its business, is to run a sound establishment. Of equal concern should be its interest in the welfare and the development of the community. Through its willingness to cooperate in making loans for sound and legitimate purposes, and its participation in those projects which contribute to the economic stability of the community, the American National Bank abundantly fulfills those cardinal tenets of excellent management."

The obvious path forward is to grow the bank through internal organic investments in infrastructure and through smart acquisitions. He understood the obligation to always grow the business and "as long as we can continue our growth, we will not sell."

As with all the leaders of the bank throughout their history, community involvement was a credo of paramount importance, both philosophically and professionally. Current board members, senior managers and effectively all staff, have integrated themselves fully into community and civic organizations and associations.

Robert's involvement in so many organizations highlights the bank's motto of service above self. Hulsey has served as President and Director of the Greater Terrell United Way, Chairman of the Terrell Park Board, Board Member of the Terrell Heritage Society, Director in the Cultural Arts of

Terrell, and Director and Chairman of the Terrell Chamber of Commerce. Hulsey has also served as Director of Texas Bankers Association, Chairman of the Independent Bankers Association of Texas, Director of the Federal Home Loan Bank of Dallas, and Director of Southwestern Automated Clearing House Association. He also served as a member of the Global Accreditation Committee, which is an international accrediting body for college programs in project management. Hulsey is a past Treasurer, Vestry Member and Senior Warden for the Episcopal Church of Good Shepherd in Terrell, Texas. He currently attends St. Andrews Episcopal Church in McKinney, Texas where he has served as Vestry Member and Senior Warden. He is also a Trustee of the Episcopal Foundation of Dallas, a Trustee of the Episcopal Diocese of Dallas Corporation, and serves on the Standing Committee for the Episcopal Diocese of Dallas. Robert currently serves as President of the Terrell ISD Excellence Foundation and Vice President of the A. Fern Norville Shelter Foundation.

On May 31, 1969, Robert married Sherry Williamson at the Episcopal Church of St. Michael's and All Angels in Dallas. Robert and Sherry have two sons, Brian Gill Hulsey and Anthony Allen Hulsey.

The most telling fact of his leadership ability is the explosion of the bank's asset base. In 1989 when Robert became President, its assets were $200 million. By 2014, the bank had surpassed $2.4 billion. The strength of his leadership not only guided the bank through its successful branch expansion, but also substantially grew its loan portfolio, all while the country was enduring its toughest years since the Great Depression of the 1930s. ★

A CULTURE OF CHARACTER AND COMMITMENT

Robert A. Hulsey

The Expansion of Branch Banking

In response to the financial meltdown in the mid-1980s, the Texas Legislature finally began to allow branch expansion, but only in the same county as the bank headquarters. It was a start, and ANB sprang into action, establishing a branch in Forney. But even though growth was the main focus, management didn't want to grow simply to get bigger. They were looking for careful and thoughtful growth that would definitively improve ANB's market presence and asset value. With many of the bank's board members and employees living there and integrated within its community, Forney was an easy call and a clear success. Deciding on the where and when the next branch would open was another question.

Throughout this turbulent time, the Texas commercial banking industry had been significantly shrinking. So many stalwart banking institutions were failing in Texas that the buyers were becoming fewer and fewer. The State of Texas realized that to recover and strengthen the state's banking industry, they needed to attract large national banks in the hopes they would acquire these failed assets. But large nationals weren't particularly interested in investing in a state where only in-county branch banking was allowed. These potential buyers wanted to freely expand statewide. Finally, the need to successfully remove the dead S&Ls and banks from the road trumped the state's resistance to branch expansion and the State of Texas finally passed legislation removing the county restriction, thereby allowing branch banking across county lines and statewide. Instantly, the banking landscape changed.

With the number of banks declining from 1,800 at the end of 1985 to slightly over 1,100 in 1992, Federal regulators began aggressively seeking well-established banking institutions with a proven track record to assume control over troubled and/or failed banks. Many of the failures would lead to mergers with solid financial institutions, which in turn would convert them to branches. In no time the Feds came calling on banks like ANB with solid financials, and this time ANB was in prime position to answer the call. With the flexibility of the new law, as well as a healthy balance sheet, management established a proactive strategy of measured risk that would help them expand beyond their county lines.

The normal course of acquiring a failing or failed bank began with receiving a circular from the FDIC. This circular listed all the banks that were in trouble or closing due to insolvency. In 1989, ANB began receiving these circulars. Now the challenge was to decide what to bid on and how much to offer.

Since this would be a competitively bid situation—usually four or five banks bidding—the bank's team conducted thorough research and careful deliberations as to which institutions they should acquire. There were a lot of factors to consider: location, age of the buildings, distance from the main location in Terrell, asset size

A CULTURE OF CHARACTER AND COMMITMENT

of the failed bank, and the cost to acquire it. Most of the locations they considered were an easy extension of their established customer base. Another important factor in reviewing failing but still active banks was to ensure ANB's culture matched with the acquisition—strong character and values, and an unwavering desire for excellence. They also needed to ensure a balanced and healthy loan portfolio (after the Feds removed some of the defaulting loans) and a strong customer base with the officers involved in their communities. So in 1989, after many long days and nights of due diligence, debate and analysis, the board agreed to bid on the assets of banks in Rockwall and Wylie, and won. These would be the first acquisitions outside of the Kaufman County home base, and the hope was that an initial success would increase their confidence and confirm they had the expertise to continue expanding.

Upon acquiring a new bank, ANB was careful to integrate its culture and processes seamlessly into their new acquisition. Though it seemed fairly successful, management wanted to measure the strengths and weakness of this integration process. This would help them gain solid knowledge of where they were succeeding and where improvements were needed. They began by soliciting feedback from all newly acquired employees with a satisfaction survey. Regarding the question, "Do you think the executive management of the bank (ANB) is committed to excellence?" The overwhelming response was a "No." This shocked the Terrell bankers. What had they done wrong? How could they continue to expand through acquisitions if their vision and mission wasn't coming across clearly?

This was a wake-up call to Robert Hulsey and his management when Robert became CEO in late 1989—something had gone wrong. They needed to improve their image with the new employees, and they needed to do it fast. A team was assembled to assess possible changes within those new properties. They asked the hard questions through a survey and tackled the areas that needed improvement. Soon, the results of their hard work shined and the new employees were happy and onboard. Today the bank surveys its employees every two years and takes the feedback very seriously, looking for more ways to cultivate a healthy, fulfilling working environment. Now, it's no accident that ANB is currently one of the most valued employers in the region six years running as measured by the Dallas Morning News.

Not long after the first two acquisitions, a Crandall location was listed in a 1990 FDIC circular. Crandall offered such a good opportunity for ANB, the board jumped at the chance. The location was so prime, in fact, that the board believed this location was likely to bring out several bidders and be very competitive. Not being sure though, they decided to bring along two bids—one with pricing for a competitive bidding situation and a second bid if they were the only bidder. When they arrived at the meeting, no other bidders were present. When the bankers asked the FDIC representative who was handling the sale where the other bidders were, they were advised that American National Bank was the sole bidder. Stone-faced they nodded, reached into their briefcase and produced the appropriate bid. When the FDIC representative opened it up and saw the figure, he announced, "Congratulations! You have just purchased this bank." On the way back to the office a hearty laugh was shared by all. Robert Hulsey reflected on this time period, "When the banking industry was having problems, we were in pretty strong shape. We were able to take advantage of the opportunity and select the banks we acquired. Our strategy included expanding our borders little by little."

Though ANB did not win all of their bids, they batted around .500 and established themselves as a winner in this messy time. With the bidding game mastered, Hulsey's team put the full weight of the bank's efforts into this expansion. They first bought assets from other banking institutions in Greenville and from Bank of America in Wills Point. They then went on to merge the First National Bank

McKinney, Texas Branch Bank

of Wills Point into the Canton Banking Center, which they had picked up from Bank of Van Zandt. They scored big when they purchased some assets of Benchmark Bank, gaining branches in Greenville, Royse City, Quinlan, and Lone Oak. From Jefferson Heritage they bought the Rowlett and Rockwall branches. By the time the FDIC selloff ended, ANB had established more locations in Forney, Kaufman, McKinney, Sachse, Seagoville, Dallas Skillman and Burleson. They had exceeded their expansion goals.

With so many new locations, the leadership team was stretched. Robert Hulsey found himself presiding over this aggressive expansion, and along with Mike Cronin and Robert Messer, discovered they had a lot to learn about managing and operating a multi-facility organization. Several operational processes and systems had to be upgraded, and these required capital investments. This gave excellent opportunities for skilled employees to be promoted and advance their careers. It was both a challenging and exciting time for the bank setting the stage for years of continued growth.

ANB was on a roll, but there were more storms to be weathered as the expansion progressed. Because of their success, the board continued reaching into the largest regional markets of North Texas: Dallas County (Dallas) and Tarrant County (Fort Worth). The locations purchased were Dallas National Bank and Citizens National Bank, bringing additional branches in Fort Worth, Mansfield, North Richland Hills, and Benbrook. These acquisitions took place during the Great Recession of 2007-2008 and according to Robert Hulsey, "Our timing was inauspicious, but fortunately our solid financial position, long-term vision and steadfastness prevailed. We have turned the corner with the wind now at our back and are pleased with our progress and the growth of these new branches."

Once they reached the supersized market of Dallas and Fort Worth, ANB realized that they'd need to offer more effective and efficient services than their firmly entrenched regional competitors.

That meant their employees needed to rise to the challenge. ANB's Director Charlie Risinger said it best, "It's about the bank's employees who make the difference. The bank always seemed to have the right people in place to manage through the tough times, and today is no different. Our bank can't really compete on price, as large banking institutions always can manage to lower their price. Our bank has always been responsive to our customers, and it's our employees who differentiate our value and make it successful even when competing against the big boys."

Another bump in the road was the increased operational load from the branches. It was heavily taxing the infrastructure. Management quickly realized they needed to upgrade their

A CULTURE OF CHARACTER AND COMMITMENT

technology. Though the bank was now very adept at integrating acquisitions into the parent bank, they needed radically different software and hardware for core banking and accounting systems, particularly as both technology and banking evolved. To solve this problem in 2002, the leaders decided to invest in the implementation of entirely new and up-to-date systems. This transition would, of course, put severe stress on the banking operations, especially on the employees. Many thought it was impossible with the current resources and that more time and people were needed. But even amidst all the doubt and uncertainty, management pressed forward, rallying the troops to succeed. During the final two weeks of the software integration testing, employees holed up in hotel rooms, ate cold pizza and battled through it, proving their mettle. The software went online with hardly any problems and the bank didn't skip a beat. The herculean effort was a success!

As any CEO knows, having bright people with passion and a strong sense of dedication are essential to any successful enterprise. At American National Bank, employee talent and loyalty have been its hallmark for decades. Throughout the bank's entire career, management diligently recruited and trained for success. The result? True resiliency: when the organization is stressed to the max, the talent steps up and gets the job done. The software integration was one of many examples where the employees stepped up and ran the extra mile. And of course the most important beneficiary of their efforts was the customers, the lifeline to even more success.

It should also be mentioned that many women employees provided long and productive service to the bank throughout the years in many capacities. Joan Harris—in lending, Geraldine Wiley—operations, Ada Zoe Smith—trust, to name a few. Even today women executives grace the leadership with Sharon Lee and Kathy Howe of particular note. ★

Mike Cronin

Since its founding, American National Bank has understood the importance of relationships—both within its own ranks and between their employees and the people in the communities they serve. The interests of this bank and those of the people whose lives it touches have been, and must forever be, closely interwoven. To accomplish this goal, ANB has relied upon its leaders to set the standard of kindness, cooperation, and integrity for all others in the bank to follow. There has been no finer example of this leadership than Mike Cronin.

Michael Cronin was born on November 7, 1939, in Terrell, to a family that had long called the area home. He graduated from Terrell High School in 1958, married his sweetheart two years later, and went on to earn a Bachelor of Business Administration degree from North Texas State University, which would later be renamed the University of North Texas. Mike and his wife, Tricia, lived and raised their family in Terrell, and Mike developed even deeper roots and a constantly growing circle of connections. He would go on to become a critical component of the culture and success of the American National Bank of Texas.

His influence began in 1983 when he joined ANB as a vice president in commercial lending. He studied to be a loan officer, helping to shore up the lending department. A current lending officer, James Springer, would soon retire, and Mike would take his place.

He quickly demonstrated his ability in the marketplace, and the reach of his network—the strong connections he had forged with the citizens, organizations, and government officials in Terrell and Kaufman County—quickly became apparent as well. When the Economic Development organization was being planned, Robert Hulsey approached Mike to join its board, believing with his vast circle of relationships that he would be best suited to move this newly developed organization forward.

Mike brought far more to the table than an impressive Rolodex, though. His character qualities were precisely what Robert and others in the bank valued, and exactly what ANB needed to thrive. Mike held an unwavering commitment to the bank's employees, the customers, and the community, the genuine kind that can't be faked—and all of them responded to it. Those who knew him well said that Mike did the right thing simply because it was the right thing to do. A gentleman to all, he expected a high standard from others and held himself to it as well. Being quiet and gentle-natured, Mike could easily disarm a tense situation or shepherd others into giving their best effort through his positive feedback and encouragement. This genuine caring and integrity brought Mike wide respect and appreciation in the community, and it helped to shape the ongoing culture of the bank—for the better.

With his character, experience, and skill, it's unsurprising that Mike moved up the ladder. When Robert Hulsey became president in 1989, Mike assumed more responsibilities as Senior Vice President of Lending, and he was then promoted to Senior Lending Officer. The bank prospered under Mike's influence.

In 1989, ANB expanded into branch banking. The first two cities, Rockwall and Wylie, Texas, were managed by seasoned employees of these branches. However, as the bank's expansion into additional cities progressed further, these branches' integration into ANB became more complex. Mike was tasked with managing the rapid expansion and integration of these branches, blending their cultures with ANB's while smoothing over issues and concerns to earn the buy-in of these newly acquired employees. He took this task in stride, and his personality was the perfect fit for a stressful time. In fact, many of these acquired branch employees said they stayed on because of Mike's personality and caring nature.

Mike was very detail oriented, ensuring that matters were always done right, and this thorough approach was needed on the board of directors. Mike assumed the title of Vice Chairman in 2002, assisting Robert and Riter Hulsey in managing the board and its strategy. As Vice Chairman, Mike served as a sounding board and buffer for the other board members and offered wise advice and direction on sensitive issues.

When Mike oversaw a project, he worked diligently to get all aspects of that project aligned and working together, whether in the industry, the city, or the county government. Mike solidified the cooperation of the whole community to face the relevant issues, and this unity and collaboration was a hallmark of his success. Two perfect examples are his involvement with the Terrell Economic Development Board in Terrell and the Terrell ISD Excellence Foundation.

In 1989, the Texas legislature allowed the citizens of a city or county to pass a sales tax to fund economic development. Mike helped to form a PAC to raise money to get this bill passed, and he generated interest from the community to ensure the bill would benefit from public approval.

Terrell was an early adapter and therefore one of the first Texas cities to benefit from the new sales tax—only the thirteenth in the state. After the bill was passed, Mike helped to form the Terrell Economic Development Corporation, which began operations in 1990. He had been involved in the Terrell Industrial Foundation, which was no longer financially workable but operated as the precursor to the EDC.

Once formed, the board of the EDC thought, "We got this money, now what are we going to do with it?" Mike had a plan.

What Terrell lacked was a developed business park with land to encourage companies to build there. Mike's vision was to secure several hundred acres and transform this land into an industrial park. Exuding confidence and professionalism to everyone, he successfully secured two business parks with fifteen hundred acres for this purpose.

Under Mike's leadership, the EDC successfully relocated thirty-five businesses to Terrell, including five Fortune 500 companies, bringing with them almost 3,600 jobs and $300 million in additional tax revenue. Notable businesses include Wal-Mart (their refrigeration and freezer division), Goodyear, AutoZone, Nucor Steel, Illinois Tool Works, and the Carlisle Group.

Mike was the natural choice to be the first chairman of the EDC, and during his twenty years of service there he was reelected every year. With the depth of his connections to the community at all levels, he was well suited to leading the EDC through two decades of city growth and development.

He was also the driving force behind restructuring the waning Chamber of Commerce, and with his efforts and funds from ANB the Chamber regained its strength. Initially the Chamber generally regulated economic development, but once the sales tax passed, some of this influence was wielded by the EDC. The Chamber controls the EDC in Terrell now, and while it's unusual that this structure exists, it works well. Both the Chamber and the city's economy have been greatly strengthened due to Mike's efforts, another result of his diligence and the force of his vision. In 2015, the tax collection that was begun in 1990 will bring in $2.5 million.

Mike's efforts benefited the community in other ways, as well. In the mid-1990s there were a number of dilapidated drug houses, and in a shared effort with Robert Hulsey and Danny Booth, Mike worked with the City of Terrell, Kaufman County, and the Terrell ISD to waive their taxing authority. These lots where the dilapidated houses had stood were then given to qualified home owners. With an approved builder, the ANB financed 100 percent of the construction, and the lot was free and clear. Over a dozen houses were constructed through this collaboration. More would have been built, but the supply of these decrepit houses ran out.

Mike also got the banking industry engaged with the Terrell ISD Excellence Foundation, which is a nonprofit organization that promotes and funds effective programs and ideas in the Terrell

LEFT to RIGHT: Don Robinson, Robert Hulsey, Ken Lane, Mike Cronin, Riter Hulsey.

Independent School District. The Foundation is dedicated to supporting excellence in education for students in Terrell. Mike, always looking for ways to increase collaboration and community involvement, worked with the Foundation on fundraising, curriculum, and support from the industry.

In addition to being deeply invested in the community, Mike shared his wisdom and guidance with his colleagues in the banking industry. He excelled in mentoring employees and was amply qualified—tactful, prompt, organized, encouraging, and perceptive.

One example of an employee who benefited from this arrangement is Casey Stewart, now Market President for ANB. Casey was working for Bank of America in Greenville when Mike visited them in 1996 to inform them that their branch was being acquired by ANB. Casey was a part-time teller and still going to college. They took a mutual liking to each other, and Mike encouraged Casey to continue working at the bank. Casey has shared that he stayed with the bank after graduation because of Mike.

Mike took a special interest in mentoring young Casey, not merely in procedures but in values. Mike guided and supported Casey through his rise to prominence. Casey commented, "Mike Cronin is the heart of the bank. He had this uplifting spirit. He genuinely cared about me and wanted me to succeed. There were times when I was impatient, and he always looked out for my career path and told me that good things will happen if I am patient."

Casey continued, "He was the type of person that enjoyed being on the front lines, listening to the employees and their concerns, encouraging and motivating. His hands-on approach made him the conscience of the bank. He was the eyes and ears to the senior leadership about what was going on in the field or in the branch banks. He never lost touch with making the bank a success because he cared so much about all employees."

This gentle touch would prove of vital importance during the economic collapse of 2008–2009. "Mike re-doubled his efforts to help the lenders in the field to work through those upside-down, bad loan situations," Casey said. "Sure, losses mounted, but it could have been a lot worse, and many bank lenders and customers might have walked out the door if not for Mike's guiding and calm presence and help."

Along with his gentle nature, though, Mike was extremely competitive—particularly on the golf course. Before the game, he made a big show of lamenting how bad he was at golf, but that all changed once he got on the first tee. He did not even have a problem waging a bet on the course with his pastor, although it was never about the money—the real prize for Mike was getting to proclaim that he won.

Mike followed a personal dedication to honesty and keeping his promises, but he also had a great sense of humor, and there was one point when these personality traits came into conflict. He always—at least, almost always—kept his promises, but one story was simply too funny to keep it secret as he had sworn to do.

The incident began with an elk hunting trip that Robert Messer took in Colorado. Unfortunately, instead of shooting an elk, Messer mistakenly shot a moose! Knowing it was the right thing to do, he decided to come clean and tell the game warden of his error. The warden didn't take lightly to this and told Messer: "Normally a person serves jail time for such an atrocious action. But in this case we'll just take a check." Messer smiled in relief, but a moment later the warden revealed the substantial amount of the fine and told Messer, "And we need this check today… and it better not bounce!"

Knowing he lacked the necessary funds in his checking account to cover such a hefty fine, Messer called Mike Cronin to arrange a transfer of funds. Mike was pleased to help bail him out, so to speak, but Messer had an additional request: "Please don't tell anyone about this!"

"Of course I won't," Mike reassured him. He abided with Messer's financial request, and he also didn't tell anyone. Rather, he told everyone! The temptation to share what had happened—for the amusement of all—was simply too great.

After Messer returned from Colorado, an employee picked him up at the airport, and Messer was relieved when nothing was mentioned on the ride to the bank about his moose-killing misadventures. He sighed in relief, knowing that Mike Cronin had kept his promise, as he always did.

This relief died the moment Messer reached his office, which now looked like a gallery of moose memorabilia! A large moose picture placed prominently on the wall. Moose streamers hanging everywhere. A message from Rocky expressing his worry that Bullwinkle was missing. Messer's nameplate on his desk had been changed to "Robert Mooser." A moose hat was strategically placed on his desk, along with some fake dung. Cases of Moosehead beer were placed throughout his office. It was Moose-a-palooza!

Some of these moose gifts became prized possessions to Messer. In fact, he went on to wear his treasured moose hat on a skiing trip. When he fell and landed hard on the slopes, nearby skiers came to check on him. Fearing that when the medics arrived they would laugh at him, Messer told the bystanders, "Just take my moose hat off!"

A CULTURE OF CHARACTER AND COMMITMENT

That was Mike Cronin's influence—even on the occasion that he failed to keep a secret, it became a cherished memory that built a stronger sense of camaraderie and community.

Of course, one of the greatest legacies anyone can leave exists in the memories he leaves with those who knew him. Riter Hulsey called Mike a "great banker and great friend to our customers and the community." Chris Cronin, Mike's son and Executive Vice President at American National Bank, shared this: "Robert Hulsey was the visionary, and Mike was the nuts and bolts personality. All he came in contact with deserved respect, and he dealt with integrity to all."

Chris went on: "As his son, he shared with me that if you're supervising people you want to be successful, then you better take ownership of your teams and have them buy into your desires. The only way to manage successfully and be a success is if your team wants you to be successful. Every time I saw my father in a situation, he always migrated to do the right thing, with integrity and always above board. He practiced what he preached."

Robert Messer called "the human side" Mike's strength and explained how Mike was careful to never forget about preserving other people's dignity.

"He was the forebear of the modern-day culture at American National Bank," Messer said. "The main driver of the long-term profitability of ANB is the culture. If the right people stay, only then will the bank make better business decisions. It starts with getting good people to join and then stay. Corporate culture is driven by individual character, and Mike had as much to do with shaping the company as all the leaders."

Messer shared the following story that illustrates the unique perspective that Mike contributed. About twenty years ago, ANB was looking for ways to strengthen the management ranks and improve the friction developed from their rapid expansion into branch banking. A consultant was hired to lead a role-playing exercise. In Messer's group, the role-play situation involved a fictitious company whose founder was ill, and now his son was taking over the company. All the participants developed questions for the son, directed toward how he could improve the company, and all were asked to state their questions. Almost everyone's questions revolved around business strategies and tactics. However, one person did not discuss business matters at all—he had a different focus. One person deemed the human element more important. That was Mike Cronin.

Mike only asked one question: "How is your father doing?" He understood that business is about people, and the personal side is a more critical part of business than anything else. After all, the son's greatest concern was not how to manage and improve the company but rather the ill health of his father.

Messer shared: "In the last three years we have had some new board members, and Mike repeatedly would ask them, 'Do you like what is going on?' 'Do you understand what is happening?', or 'We really appreciate your input and direction.' Mike's strength was to think of others first, a service-above-self mentality."

Mike retired from the bank in 2006 but remained very active by serving as Vice Chairman of the Board of Directors. He served on numerous other boards throughout his professional career, which included Board Chairman of the Trinity River Authority, Chairman of the Terrell Chamber of Commerce, Founding President of the Terrell Economic Development Corporation, and a board member of the Terrell ISD Excellence Foundation. He was also a member of the First United Methodist Church of Terrell and held many leadership positions at the church, serving the congregation and the community.

Mike Cronin

Chris Cronin summed up what many others have expressed about his father: "It was always about the people."

Mike Cronin passed away after a short illness on November 14, 2015. He made a significant difference, both in his community and at American National Bank, and he will be greatly missed. ★

Expanding the Services

With the expansion of new branches taking the bank to tremendous growth levels, business exploded. Customers loved the culture of community banking where they could develop strong relationships with people they knew and saw often. Yet ANB soon realized that more services were needed for three reasons: to expand their customer base, to meet their ever-growing needs, to keep the competition at bay.

In 1995, the first idea was to provide free checking. Many were concerned there would not be enough new accounts generated from this idea to be profitable, but their concerns were quickly dispelled. The free checking was a huge success and brought in a lot of new business. Free was good, and the customer base grew at a pace surprising even the leadership.

Then in 2000, community banking—always a hallmark of ANB—began losing customers. The culprit was the lure of credit cards. Companies like GMAC began making more car loans and, since they already had a customer making payments to them, sold them a credit card. These captive finance companies sent ANB's two revenue sources—interest from loans and service fees—into a decline, which in turn caused a slight downward trend in profitability. Management knew that adding new branches was not the answer to this particular conundrum—they needed to come up with something new. The trick was finding something that provided services customers wanted while at the same time generated revenue for the bank. They also needed to consider which services, if ANB did not provide them, would send customers elsewhere. It was as much about being on the defensive as it was about being on the offensive.

To that end, over the years the bank added telephone banking, call center assistance, online banking and eventually a mobile App to its portfolio of services to further benefit its customers.

The bank also decided that phasing in more trust services and offering insurance products and brokerage services was a good place to start.

Trust services were not a new concept. ANB had been providing trust and investment services to their clientele since 1926. They had become very adept at managing and distributing assets consistent with the intent of the settlor and were also experienced at carefully administering trust holdings while clearly communicating with the beneficiaries. Even though these services existed, they hadn't been advertised or pushed. To ramp them up, they added staff to handle the workload and trained the various branches to sell the services. Currently, the bank has an excellent trust and estate department, which benefits both its clients and adds to the bank's bottom line.

In line with ramping up its trust and estate services, ANB next decided to offer wealth management services. The bank hired experts who could staff this new "Wealth Management Group" and provide excellent counsel, as well as sound investment plans in stocks, bonds, mutual funds and annuities. It didn't take long before they were adept at offering investment portfolio analysis for both individual and corporate customers alike. Then, in 2012, the bankers implemented yet another new service: managing small business customers' 401K plans.

In 2003, management uncovered a need for even more services: personal insurance, commercial insurance, health insurance and risk management services. A thorough study of all this revealed that property and casualty services would be a valuable addition too. As such, they began seeking a company to acquire, one with the right ethics and culture. Eventually they targeted Sleeper Sewell Insurance Services, Inc., a company that looked promising. After completing the purchase, they found integrating the two companies was more difficult than they had thought. Some key executives from the acquired firm departed further adding to this problem. Undaunted, ANB pressed forward, eventually reaching a nice portfolio balance with property and casualty comprising 65% and health insurance the remaining 35%. According to Robert Hulsey, all of these services have become a valuable addition to the bank's overall performance, bringing in both growth and profits, "Insurance has a good runway ahead, especially as we have scaled the business and it's an important value added service in our portfolio."

In addition to the expansion of these services, management worried about their core principle of relationship banking. Historically, the bank's employees have always held a passion to help people, to create value for their customers and to build lasting personal relationships. In fact relationship banking had served ANB well for so many years. Yet with all the changes in technology, the addition of internet banking and the regulatory environment, they were concerned that customer relationships were being minimized. Was this happening? Was ANB still relationship focused? The bankers needed answers. To get them, they hired the consulting firm Starizon.

Starizon's job was to analyze various scenarios, all focused on small-to-medium sized business customers. They would dive deep and answer these two questions: "Who are we?" and "What improvements are needed in our value proposition to enhance relationship banking and our customer experience?" Starizon's findings pushed the bank to seek even more data.

When Deluxe Corporation initiated a focus group with twelve banks to analyze this same small business market segment, Robert Hulsey jumped at the chance to participate. The Deluxe findings indicated that for the most part, banks were long on knowledge but short on relationship building. Small businesses wanted a trusted advisor, one who went beyond the transactional elements. Robert Hulsey summarized their conclusions by stating, "This shed light on what American National had become. We realized that this was exactly who we were. We have used this strategic model to adapt and establish relationships and execute accordingly. We used this for both retail and commercial employing a high discovery phase with our customers." This information generated a renewed focus on understanding the customer's needs. Each branch aggressively pursued finding out what their customers wanted. Robert added, "This builds goodwill and helps us understand how we can help them."

After this discovery phase, management discussed the findings and looked for more ways they could build better relationships with its customers. Walter Allen, a past leader, used to say, "A relationship is not about one more loan. It's about understanding one more

A CULTURE OF CHARACTER AND COMMITMENT

aspect of your business partner. Relationships come first, then the business will come for the benefit of all." One recommendation from the Deluxe study was to further integrate ANB's employees into the business communities where their branches were situated, especially the remote locations. Today, these local branches have implemented a business development board. These boards are filled with trusted businessmen—professionals who are experts and uniquely qualified to assist ANB's enterprise customers, both small and large. And of course, all of this further integrates ANB's people deeper into the community.

While other banks focus on the time value of money, the Terrell bankers have always understood the money value of time. Steadfast in their conservative lending practices, they are equally interested in their communities and calculate ROI not only as Return on Investment but as Return on Involvement. ★

How to Make $20 Trillion Disappear: The Great Recession of 2008-2009

The real estate boom spanning 2000-2006 created a host of opportunities for every U.S. lending institution. Almost every one of them took full advantage and American National Bank was no exception. The market was white hot and the federal government fueled the fire by revisiting the Community Reinvestment Act of 1977, which required banks to take on substantially greater risk by offering mortgages to even the most marginally qualified. Given that this was federal law, the banks had to abide by these regulations. Refusing would have meant inviting the Feds, at their discretion, to impose demands (including fines). This put pressure on the banks to provide even more housing loans, whether they were justified or not.

Soon, unique mortgages appeared: interest-only mortgages where the borrower paid no principal whatsoever; no-down- payment loans where the borrower had no skin in the game; loans to borrowers who had FICO scores below 600 (which meant they had real trouble managing their own finances); undocumented income loans where a nail technician was able to swear they annually earned $300,000 without any verification whatsoever; and liberal debt-to- income ratios where a borrower owed lenders a huge percentage of what they earned. All of these "subprime loans" (as they were termed) were simply ingredients in a poisonous cocktail that just about every financial institution drank. Most of these loans were packaged into securities and sold to investors who gobbled them up for the excellent yields. However, all of these investors, including the U.S. government, were basically holding paper that was about to go up in flames. With such ultra-liberal lending policies, the chances of a mass default were sky high, but no one was paying attention—the housing market was booming, and everyone was taking advantage of it, including American National Bank. Those flames, when they came, would test all financial institutions, both great and small.

In 2005 ANB joined the fray. Between the loose lending terms, the unstoppable deals, and being pressured by the Fed, ANB got caught up in the surge and made some fundamental underwriting mistakes during this time. As with many other financial institutions, sales got in front of the loan approval process, and by breezing through the initial loan application process and without the appropriate loan oversight or capital to backstop defaults, ANB found itself overextended. "Our most severe issues arose from a commercial lending group which was pretty aggressive on commercial properties and speculative endeavors such as strip centers," said Riter Hulsey. Fortunately, Riter and his management team recognized this and took preemptive action.

By early 2006, the ANB bankers foresaw a market collapse on the near horizon and were among the first to eliminate subprime lending. This was a huge decision, as the real estate market had begun to freefall and investors were scrambling for the exits. Fortunately, when the bubble burst in 2007, ANB had already begun realigning its lending practices. They also retreated from their portfolio of weaker land development positions, refusing to write additional loans for those areas.

Another way ANB buckled down their risks, was to study a number of their loans on large commercial retail and office entities—significant investments with large exposures for the bank. These were not like their traditional customers of the past, which had always been based on relationship banking. With relationship banking, they knew their customers and made it their goal to help them succeed. These commercial loans were the opposite—transaction-based investments with little or no initial relationship and none ever developed. It turned out that these relationships were key: without a substantive relationship, it was difficult to analyze a customer's position and see how they would perform. Realizing they couldn't fully understand the depth of their customers' exposure and thus, the downside risk, they quickly backed away from these overleveraged customers. If they were stuck in a deal and unable to work through a restructuring or "workouts," the bank aggressively foreclosed, minimizing their loss.

Finally, the bank took advantage of a government program created for this situation—The Troubled Asset Relief Program (TARP). In this program, the United States government purchased assets and equity from financial institutions to help strengthen the financial sector. Because TARP could stabilize bank capital ratios, it allowed American National Bank to increase lending instead of hoarding all its cash to cushion against future unforeseen losses from troubled assets. Increased lending equated to a loosening of credit, which the government hoped would restore order to the financial markets and improve investor confidence in both the financial institutions and the markets. Though only 12% of the bank's total asset base was invested in these higher risk commercial real estate deals, the deterioration of the market alarmed management and the bank decided to bring in Mike Gunnels to restructure these assets and tap $20 million from TARP. Even though TARP had onerous terms, the bank was unsure of where the bottom might be and felt that these TARP funds would be a safe backstop to de-risk their positions.

As effective as they eventually were, these remedial actions could not happen overnight and reversing the effect on the bank of the collapse of the real estate market took years. And while banks in the U.S. were still reeling, the worst financial crisis since the Great Depression of the 1930s—the Global Financial Crisis—was headed right for them.

Also known as the Great Recession of 2007-2008, the Global Financial Crisis left no country in the developed world unaffected. Around the world large financial institutions threatened to collapse, national governments felt forced to bailout banks that were "too big to fail," and stock markets plunged. In most areas of the U.S., the housing market blowout was in full swing. This resulted in massive evictions and foreclosures, sending millions to the unemployment rolls as construction virtually dried up overnight. As the Great Recession spread, it resulted in prolonged unemployment in a number of key business sectors along with more companies going under. It didn't take long before trillions of dollars in consumer wealth was lost and the world was thrust into economic darkness.

The autopsy on the cause of this great economic calamity reveals a perfect storm that began with the bursting of the U.S. housing bubble, which peaked in 2006. This caused the value of securities tied to U.S. real estate pricing to plummet, severely damaging many of the largest financial institutions globally. Some of the biggest names in the industry either folded or had to be bought out. Hundreds, if not thousands, of smaller banks and mortgage brokers shut their doors. The financial crisis was intensified by a complex interaction of policies that were almost impossible to disentangle from each other. Home ownership was being encouraged, which provided easier access to loans for the aforementioned subprime borrowers. This allowed for the overvaluation of bundled subprime mortgages, based on the theory that housing prices would continue to climb. Now add to this mix numerous questionable trading practices on behalf of both buyers and sellers of real estate-backed securities, a number of compensation structures that rewarded short-term deal making over long-term value creation, and a lack of adequate capital within banks and insurance companies to back the financial commitments they were making, and you get one fine, complicated mess. With numerous banks teetering on collapse, no credit to be had for investors, and damaged investor confidence, the global stock markets were struck hard and their securities suffered huge losses during 2008 and early 2009. Economies worldwide slowed during this period, as credit tightened and international trade declined. Governments and central banks responded with unprecedented fiscal stimulus packages, monetary policy expansion and institutional bailouts. In the U.S., Congress passed the American Recovery and Reinvestment Act of 2009.

Many have weighed in on the root cause for the financial crisis. The U.S. Senate's Levin-Coburn Report asserted that the crisis was the result of "high risk, complex financial products; undisclosed conflicts of interest; the failure of regulators, the credit rating agencies, and the market itself to rein in the excesses of Wall Street." Many believed that the 1999 repeal of the Glass- Steagall Act (which effectively removed the separation between investment banks and depository banks in the United States) was an aggravating factor. Critics have also argued that credit rating agencies and investors failed to accurately price the risk involved with mortgage-related financial products, and that the government did not adequately adjust their regulatory practices to address modern financial markets. Research into the causes of the financial crisis has also focused on the role of interest rate spreads. For every expert, there's a different cause.

As for American National Bank, by 2007 it was obvious that serious problems were mounting and the bankers knew they had to attack them fast to get ahead of the downward spiral. At the same time, they were committed to remaining competitive. It wouldn't be easy and it would take time. Many initiatives were put in place over the next two years to repair the damage and recover from the shock to the industry. The bankers' goals were to assure stability, and then identify key steps they could take for future growth.

First, they needed a full stress analysis. Where were the issues? What was the downside risk? How quickly could they reframe the opportunities and recover? Though it wasn't do or die, it was still all hands on deck. They needed the best analysis and worst-case scenarios in order to establish a good plan to shore up any leaks and still provide for adequate sailing.

Next, they took the answers and information and sat down to formulate a strategic plan, one that would not just limit the exposures, but would also place ANB on a profitable path that would last well into the 21st century. This strategic plan had to continue long-term growth yet be flexible and innovative. And they needed to retain their market share while maintaining their trusted position in the community.

A CULTURE OF CHARACTER AND COMMITMENT

Third, past experience told them the best policy was an open and honest disclosure to the overseers: the Feds. They needed to advise them of the problems and seek whatever counsel the Feds could provide. With that in mind, in 2007 the bankers of ANB requested a meeting with the Deputy Comptroller of the Currency in Dallas to discuss the situation. Because of their national charter, The Comptroller of the Currency, under the U.S. Treasury, is the regulatory authority under which ANB is governed. This bold step was unusual, as generally such meetings are called by the Feds. But the conservative and honest ANB bankers knew from the past that an aggressive strategy of truthfulness and full disclosure was their best policy in dealing with the Feds. As Robert Hulsey remembers, "We knew the best tactic was to come clean and advise the authorities what we were facing. As the OCC (Office of the Comptroller of the Currency) could be very heavy-handed, we knew a proactive approach would bode well for our relationship with them."

At the meeting with OCC's Gil Barker, the bank had laid out their three-year view of asset quality, earnings and capital requirements. The bankers were clear that the bottom had not yet been hit, but that it was in sight. They were confident, based on their plan, that a turn-around was workable, and they could hit the needed numbers in time to resolve all issues. They believed that their recovery would be strong. Very surprised to hear all this, the OCC mentioned they never had a bank call them up requesting a meeting to share bad news. Never. Because the bankers of ANB were honest and proactive and had initiated the "coming clean" process, they were allowed more time to work through the failed loans. Though these were wrenching times, they worked their way through the recovery and always kept the OCC informed. Because of this, the OCC was continually fair to them and preserved their relationship in good standing. This was a stark contrast to what many of their less forthright competitors faced.

Another characteristic that served the bankers of ANB well during this time was the ability to react quickly. Throughout their history, the bank has had an internal credo that "bad news needs to travel at warp speed." As Robert Messer likes to say, "The bank has an unwritten policy: If you have good news, grab a cup of coffee and walk down the hall and tell management. If you have bad news, skip the coffee and run down here." Their willingness to deal with problems as fast as possible and to do whatever it took to correct it, enabled them to get ahead of the potential financial tsunami and lessen the downside impact. They did what was necessary, biting the bullet early to minimize losses.

In the end, ANB's true saving grace was found in their stable earnings set solidly on top of a strong deposit base. This allowed them to set aside a significant amount of capital for failed loans, giving them time to reverse their negative positions. Typically a bank will set aside 1% to 1.5% of assets to cover failed loans. ANB had always maintained a 2% threshold and this provided an air bag large enough to survive the crash. Luckily the bank actually had a lot less real estate loans than their competitors, so the damage was less impactful than what others were facing. "When the bottom fell out we had some problems in our loan portfolio, but fundamentally the bank had advantages over our peers," said Robert Messer, Chief Financial Officer.

There was a point during the recovery when management asked for a report to assess customer loan risks. The report came back with dozens of customers highlighted in yellow. When asked why there were so many highlighted customers, the report's producer said, "These are our former customers that are now bankrupt!" This was a sign of the times, but unlike many of their former customers and competitors, ANB made it through. As Riter Hulsey reflected back on the economic recession of 2008, he stated, "It has made my memory awfully good on some bad decisions. One can only gain experience from making ill-advised loans, and that we did, but fortunately we managed successfully to learn from these errors and strengthened our balance sheets to ensure sustainability forward."

Staying proactive and understanding both their customers' and the market's direction—no matter how it might affect the balance sheet—was the character and hallmark of the bank. It had proven to be the key to its survival during times of crisis. The bank had always done what was right (no matter how painful) to correct an erroneous position and ensure long-term stability for its stakeholders. After all, it was their principled leaders of the past who had passed on these foundational values to current management. It was what had served them so well for 140 years and undoubtedly will continue to do so.

By the time the dust settled, disaster had clearly been averted, but the bank was somewhat bruised. "We fortunately recovered well and still retained our employees," said Riter Hulsey. "We shored up our balance sheets, our relationship with the Feds, and realigned our percentages of quality loans to substandard loans. We had a lot of good people to help us out of this difficult situation and made the right decisions on a timely basis." Since the beginning of the economic downturn, each quarter the bank maintained positive earnings, increased capital, and improved reserves, all while delivering exceptional service to its customers.

In the immediate aftermath of the financial crisis, the Dodd-Frank regulatory reforms were enacted to lessen the chance of a recurrence. This new regulatory structure required that more resources would be needed to comply with the law—more people, more infrastructure, and more costs. As an example, ten years ago the bank had one person handling compliance. Now fifteen were required. More costs and expenses put pressure on fee services and forced a tightening of profit margins. ANB realized the pendulum had just swung from a moderately regulated financial industry with quite liberal lending policies to one that many perceive as overkill. And this was put in place after most, if not all, the financial institutions that were less prudent had already gone under. What probably started out as a well-intended effort to protect the consumer, turned out to have unintended consequences in placing substantial burdens on the surviving financial institutions. And of course, the customers are the ones who have to share these costs and meet new loan qualification hurdles. Financial institutions now find themselves in a world where only the well capitalized and ethically grounded can possibly flourish. For those in this industry who may think they can continue to play around the edges and take a "business as usual" approach to the present regulatory landscape, the future is…well…not so bright. And for those waiting around for things to get back to normal, the fact is, this is the new normal.

ANB, having realized that early on, came to grips with the situation and has adjusted quite well.

What was the next hurdle? Figuring out how to comply with all the new banking regulations and electronic changes the new oversight created. Research showed that compliance was going to have a severe impact on the customers, so the question then became: How to manage all this in a logical and cost effective way with the least impact on service? One key way was to invest in online banking. With the explosion of the Internet, online banking was growing rapidly and had become a necessity to their customer base. Both business and individual customers wanted more reporting of their transactions. They also wanted fraudulent protection and remote deposit capability. For both the bank and its customers, this significant development reduced costs, provided more timely transactions, and expanded the bank's ability to serve customers from anywhere.

Again, to facilitate this transition they turned to upgrading their software and hardware infrastructure. In 2012, significant resources were directed to enhance their technology platforms and expand their technology groups. Moving beyond the Internet and telecommunications, the idea was to use information and systems to orchestrate a symbiotic partnership between the various branches and regulators, while simultaneously aligning with what their customers wanted. These pieces were critical to the bank's future in developing superior technology for both their customers and their internal processes.

The wildly turbulent years of the Great Recession were indeed trying, but in the end ANB did what was right and not only survived, but thrived. As they had for 140 years, they continued to exhibit a passion for creating value and delivering excellence.

The road ahead for American National Bank, though in some ways uncertain, is firmly positioned to continue their legacy to surmount any economic peril that may lie ahead. ★

Robert Hulsey and team receiving The Principle
10 Best Companies Award in 2012

Board of Directors

Certainly of paramount importance through the success and travails of the bank over its many years of continued service has been the unfaltering leadership and vision of its board members.

These individuals used their expertise and experience to provide ANB with governance, policy direction and strategic planning.

Typical duties of boards of directors include:

- governing the organization by establishing broad policies and objectives;
- selecting, appointing, supporting and reviewing the performance of the chief executive;
- ensuring the availability of adequate financial resources;
- approving annual budgets;
- accounting to the stakeholders for the organization's performance; and
- setting the salaries and compensation of company management.

In addition, its members were ever mindful that banks, the safeguard of the free enterprise system, traditionally have been expected to foster industry with money to finance business growth, economic expansion, rising employment, and to better conditions of the consuming public. Throughout the bank's long history, its board members' stewardship of these funds, entrusted to it by all segments of the community, remained sound, thus vindicating the trust the community placed in it. The board performed their functions, which justified its existence.

With a value system of serving the needs of individuals and being persons of exceptional character, the community of Terrell and surrounding cities were built on their shoulders. All board members throughout these generations took an active leadership role in the community. The board members, more or less, controlled the flow of money and the area's economic lifeblood. The success of the bank and the areas it served are a testament to these men's ability, dedication, loyalty and leadership.

The Board of Directors' key variables through its history that have provided a strong bank for its customers and a solid investment for our stockholders have been the following:

- The board has a tradition of shifting from growth to turnaround management in the hour of crisis, without the upheaval of turnover. They made decisions together, confronted problems together, and solved them together. Loyalty was a key ingredient in a survival recipe that did not include scapegoating, revolving doors, pointing fingers, and wholesale changes.
- They had the foresight to correct mistakes before they got out of hand. When overaggressive lending on real estate in the 1980s occurred, the bank corrected them

swiftly, limiting the long- term impact.
- With branch expansion in the 1980s and 1990s, the board was careful not to allow too much decentralization and ensured a process in place for closely supervised loan review and other critical aspects of the business.

The key variable of the board's success, and hence the bank's, was its ability to always focus on the long-term, instead of expedient and popular views they could have taken. As states Robert Hulsey of this generational influence: "A vast majority of our stockholders can trace their stock back to the turn of the century. Many board members are gifting stock to their children. This continuity allows us to focus long-term on what is in the best interests for customers, employees and the bank."

As well, their compassion should not be overlooked. Many times the board would open their personal pockets to help out a family, especially an employee or their children. This giving and caring nature has been a telling character quality of the bank's board members.

Every bank board has different personalities with a mixture of experiences and strengths. The commonality of ANB's board is that they are all very engaged, they do their homework, come prepared and are very involved and focused, as well have a plethora of entrepreneurial backgrounds with a deep understanding of business, goals, direction and vision for the future.

Today the Board of Directors is made up of a diversified group of business people from all areas we serve. This provides insight into the needs of the customers. Many of these board members were very colorful figures with strong characters, equally strong willed and, though very opinionated, have

Board of Directors, 1950

always managed to come together when a decision needed to be rendered. Very few times has any member stood up and objected once the decision was made. Even when mistakes were made, they worked together to ensure a clear path forward.

The board leadership had historically been very stable. Currently its board members have tenured an average of thirty years. This is a remarkable legacy and their experience, dedication, and thoroughness have long served as a valuable foundation for the bank and will undoubtedly continue to ensure its success in the years to come.

Current Board of Directors

J. W. Barrow, III has been a director of American National Bank since January 12, 1982. He currently serves on the Directors Executive Committee, Directors Loan Committee, Examining & Trust Audit Committee (Chair), Facilities Committee, Credit Committee, Risk Committee, and Insurance Committee. J. W. is a retired businessman.

A CULTURE OF CHARACTER AND COMMITMENT

William D. Breedlove has been an advisory director of ANB since October 2003. He serves on the Examining & Trust Audit Committee.

Guinn F. Godwin became a director of American National Bank January 20, 1976. He retired from the bank in March 31, 1985, but continues to serve in a business development capacity. On March 17, 1987, Guinn became an Advisory Director and continues to serve on the board.

Riter C. Hulsey became a director of American National Bank on January 11, 1949. He was named Chairman of the Board on December 13, 1983. Riter continues to work at the bank, serving on many committees.

Robert A. Hulsey became a director of American National Bank on June 9, 1981. Robert serves as the President and CEO of the bank since named to that position in October 1989.

James B. McGinty, III has been a director of American National Bank since January 15, 1991. He serves on the Directors Executive Committee, Directors Loan Committee, Asset/Liability Management Committee, Wealth Management Committee, Credit Committee, Risk Committee, and Facilities Committee (Chair). Jim is a retired local businessman.

Ann D. Melsheimer has been a director of American National Bank since August 19, 2003. She currently serves on the Directors Executive Committee, Directors Loan Committee, Asset/Liability Management Committee, Compensation Committee, Credit Committee, Risk Committee, and Technology Committee (Chair). Ann is a retired businesswoman.

AMERICAN NATIONAL BANK

Deceatur B. Mitchell, Jr. has been a director of American National Bank since March 17, 1979. He serves on the Directors Executive Committee, Directors Loan Committee, Credit Committee, Risk Committee, and Examining & Trust Audit Committee. Bob is a local businessman and rancher.

Kenneth F. Moody became a director of American National Bank on January 12, 1982. He serves on the Directors Executive Committee, Directors Loan Committee, Wealth Management Committee, Credit Committee, Risk Committee, and Insurance Committee. Kenneth is a retired businessman and rancher.

Wylie G. Musser became a director of American National Bank on January 10, 1978. He serves on the Directors Executive Committee, Directors Loan Committee, Asset/Liability Management Committee, Compensation Committee, Credit Committee, Risk Committee, Wealth Management Committee, and Examining & Trust Audit Committee. Wylie is the owner of a local car dealership.

Tom E. Norton, Jr. has been a director of American National Bank since June 11, 1968. He serves on the Directors Executive Committee (Chair), Directors Loan Committee, Asset/Liability Management Committee, Credit Committee, Risk Committee, and Facilities Committee. Tom is the owner of a local construction company.

Charlie C. Risinger has been a director of American National Bank since March 15, 2005. He currently serves on the Directors Executive Committee, Directors Loan

Committee, Directors Credit Committee, Technology Committee, Credit Committee, Risk Committee, and Wealth Management Committee. Charlie is a local medical doctor.

Larry Parks has been a director of American National Bank since September 20, 2011. He currently serves on the Directors Executive Committee, Directors Loan Committee, Asset/Liability Management Committee, Credit Committee, Risk Committee, Facilities Committee, and Wealth Management Committee. Larry is Senior Vice President of business development at American National Bank's banking center in Rockwall, and he has been with the bank for over 20 years.

Gary L. Martin has been an advisory director of American National Bank since January 21, 2014. On August 19, 2014, he was appointed full director. He currently serves on the Directors Executive Committee, Directors Loan Committee, Compensation Committee, Credit Committee, Risk Committee, and Wealth Management Committee. Gary is retired from Capital Southwest Corporation.

James R. Thompson became a director June 17, 2014. Jim currently serves on the Directors Executive Committee, Directors Loan Committee, Credit Committee, Risk Committee, Facilities Committee, and Technology Committee. He is CEO of James R. Thompson, Inc., a general contracting company. ★

Previous Board of Directors

J. H. Muckleroy	1895 to 1896
Oscar Price	1895 to 1921
J. B. Harris	1895 to 1902
Dr. A. J. Childress	1895 to 1898
J. E. McMorries	1895 to 1914
J. S. Grinnan	1895 to 1898
John H. Corley	1895 to 1913
H. H. Hickok	1895 to 1902
Robt. L. Warren	1895
J. C. Maples	1896 to 1898
H. M. Cate	1898 to 1905
E. H. R. Green	1898
W. P. Allen	1898
T. E. Corley	1902 to 1924
R. Jarvis	1902
D. M. Purvine	1905
J. C. Fields	1913 to 1916
P. J. Manning	1915 to 1922
B. E. Overton	1917
W. C. McCord	1917
M. C. Cartwright	1921
W. Charlton Griffith	1921
B. L. Gill, Sr.	1923
Ben Allen	1925

Board of Directors, 2000

Board of Directors, 2014
Standing, left to right: Ann Melsheimer, Larry Parks, James Thompson
Jim McGinty, Robert Hulsey, Mike Cronin
Tom Norton, J.W. Barrow, Wylie Musser
Charlie Risinger, Gary Martin
Kenneth Moody
Seated, left to right: Bill Breedlove, Riter Hulsey
Guinn Godwin, Bob Mitchell

Tomorrow's Opportunities

The future promises to be exceedingly bright for the American National Bank of Texas. As economic conditions improve for consumers and businesses alike, the challenge to all is to keep the momentum and focus, ensuring a better future for their customers, communities, and their stakeholders.

There must be no doubt, however, that to build upon their enviable success of the past they must continue to abide by the values that have served the bank and its customers so well for over one hundred years. Those values of service above self, fairness, dedication to excellence in everything, and delivering personalized tailored solutions to clients' needs remains necessary for the bank to prosper tomorrow. That has always been their character and commitment.

This opportunity for continued success properly rests upon the capable shoulders of its employees. Robert Hulsey continues to stress to employees that though the history and heritage of the bank is important, "it's the core values our employees possess towards people that make the difference."

Robert believes, much like the bank's leaders of the past that the bank must continue to "hire the right people first and then they will be successful, as will our institution, in whatever direction the future holds." Robert and the CEOs who preceded him would all agree that the success of any enterprise is only as strong as the character and diligence of the people who strive to deliver exceptional services and products to its customers each and every day. If there has been a consistent theme throughout this narrative it is that ANB has built its business and century-plus reputation around talented and dedicated employees who exhibit their passion for responding to their customer's needs as only ANB can. These are the people who make lemonade out of the lemons that inevitably come their way and seem to always find a path through the most difficult of circumstances. They are a very special group and ANB is honored to call them family.

There are no absolute guarantees for continued success in the years to come. After all this is an uncertain world, but what the shareholders and the communities it serves can count on is that the bank will be forward looking, adapt to change in a timely and responsive manner, and, in short, excel on all fronts. ANB will closely guard its solid fiduciary principles and provide prosperity to all they serve today and tomorrow based on their culture of character and commitment.

The bank looks forward to the challenging and exciting times ahead, and one day…far into the future…someone will relate "the rest of the story".

"After 140 years of helping thousands of businesses, individuals, and families achieve their financial goals, ANB's tradition of strong leadership and excellence inspires us to reach even higher."

—Robert A. Hulsey, President and CEO

After all, this is what got them here in the first place.